Prof. FILIPPO BOTTAZZI

Director of the Institute of Experimental Physiology
of the Royal University of Naples

-->-<+-

MEDIUMISTIC PHENOMENA

Observed in a series of sessions
with Eusapia Palladino

Translated by Irmeli Routti and
Antonio Giuditta

ICRL PRESS
PRINCETON, NEW JERSEY

Mediumistic Phenomena
By Filippo Bottazzi
Translation Copyright © 2011 by Antonio Giuditta and
Irmeli Routti
ISBN: 1-936033-05-4

Cover painting of Eusapia Palladino by Louis Malteste, 1908
Cover design by Laura Smyth

Table of Contents

Subject, Author, and Translators

Eusapia Palladino

Born in 1854 in the southern Italian town of Minervino Murge, Bari, in a family of poor farmers, Eusapia lost her mother soon after birth, and six years later her father was assassinated by brigands. As an orphan, she was sent to live with a well-to-do family in Naples, where people attempted to educate her, but with little success. Following their refusal to take further care of her, she managed to survive doing precarious jobs and with the help of other families. Later on she married a merchant of limited means. Throughout her life she remained an illiterate woman.

Her paranormal faculties came out spontaneously at the age of 13–14, when she started to give occasional demonstrations to friends. From that time, she was led to believe that her mediumistic performances were supported and controlled by a spiritual guide, John King, whom she considered to be her (new) father. Eventually she became the object of considerable interest by Neapolitan spiritists who successfully called the attention of well-known scientists to her. As a result, Eusapia was frequently examined by neurologists, psychiatrists, and members of societies devoted to the study of abnormal psychic phenomena. Her capacities were studied in numerous sessions in Italy, France, England, and the USA. Twenty-two such sessions took place in the period 1891–1908 (Carrington, 1909). Often accused of fraud and of having been found in trickery several times, her response could be of harsh indignation. Her striking personality and performances (Alvarado, 1993) also called the attention of European aristocracy, and Eusapia was often invited to princely mansions, where she was lavishly rewarded. Nonetheless, as noted by the daughter of Professor Lombroso who described Eusapia at the age of 54, she did not have "the manner of one who either poses or tricks or deceives others. She has had the perversity, a rare occurrence, to remain as nature made her: outspoken, sincere, instinctive" (Carrington, 1909, p. 21). She died in 1918.

A high proportion of the large number of anomalous phenomena Eusapia was capable of producing was considered genuine by reliable investigators. It is of interest that several well-known scientists and experts of psychical science, including Enrico Morselli, Cesare Lombroso, Camille Flammarion, Charles Richet, and Hereward Carrington, who started out highly skeptical of such events, fully admitted their genuine occurrence once they directly witnessed Eusapia's performances.

Alvarado, C. S. (1993). Gifted subjects' contributions to psychical research: the case of Eusapia Palladino. *Journal of the Society for Psychical Research*, 59, 269–292.

Carrington, H. (1909). *Eusapia Palladino and her phenomena*. London: T. Werner Laurie.

Prof. Filippo Bottazzi

Filippo Bottazzi was the most distinguished Italian physiologist of the first part of last century. Born in 1867 in a small southern town in Italy (Diso, Lecce), he obtained his MD degree and held the chair of Physiology in the university of Naples from 1904 to 1938. His "theory of sarcoplasm" was highly held for decades, and his 1898 treatise in two volumes "Chimica Fisiologica" was translated into German and was generally considered the best world book of Physiological Chemistry for years (see Prof. Lee's comments in Nature 1989). In 1923 he received the Laurea Honoris Causa at Edinburgh University. The first Italian school of Biochemistry was born because of his initiative and interest. Bottazi was fellow of sixteen scientific national and international Academies, was the rector of the University of Naples (1926–1927), member of the Consiglio Superiore Pubblica Istruzione (1926–1927), and president of the Comitato Nazionale Biologia (1937). When selected as the Italian candidate for the Nobel Prize in Medicine (1940), the Prize was suspended for the Second World War, and a year later he died in his home town.

Sharing a keen interest in the history and methodology of science, he wrote numerous studies on Leonardo da Vinci from 1902 to the eve of his death. He supported the validity of physico-chemical explanations in biological research but considered the human mind something of very different nature. He maintained that scientific prejudices are to be corrected by experimental results and theoretical acquisition, since scientific theories are open to change. In biology, he considered the comparative approach as both necessary and useful.

Antonio Giuditta

Antonio Giuditta is an MD who received his training
in neurochemistry at the Einstein College of Medicine
in New York, and for almost 40 years has headed a
summer research lab at the Marine Biological Lab in
Woods Hole, MA. He was Director of Research of the
Italian National Research Council and Full Professor
of Physiology at the Federico II University of Naples.
He retired in 2007 but is still an active investigator
in neurobiology. He has proposed and validated anti-
dogmatic concepts, including the primary involvement
of slow-wave sleep in memory processing, the partici-
pation of brain DNA synthesis in memory formation,
and the presence of local systems of gene expression

in axons and presynaptic terminals. On the theoretical side, he has long favored neo-Lamarckian views on biological evolution and is recently interested in the nature and phylogenetic origin of mind.

Irmeli Routti

Irmeli Routti is a Finnish architect from the Helsinki University of Technology. Having studied Italian in Geneva and Naples, she felt quite intrigued by the prospect of translating into English the unusual events so vividly narrated by Professor Filippo Bottazzi in his book. She hopes that her efforts will help make the evidence of those unusual biological feats and potentials available to a wider public.

Translator's Foreword

Being a good old friend of Prof. Bottazzi's grandson (Prof. Massimo Libonati), I had an occasion to discover the original 1909 edition of Bottazzi's "Fenomeni medianici" some twenty years ago. The book was lying, half ignored, on a bookshelf in Bottazzi's mansion in Diso, his birthplace, a small Italian town in the province of Lecce, Puglia. This was how I first became acquainted with Bottazzi's extraordinary experiments. He had made them in 1907 at the Royal University of Naples in order to examine the striking capacities of Eusapia Palladino, perhaps the most famous medium of her time. In later years I occasionally reread the book several times, always with amazement, but every time hindered and distracted by more pressing tasks.

Only a few years ago something happened that made things turn a different way. An unexpected invitation allowed me to participate in the 2007 European meeting of the Society for Scientific Exploration (SSE) in Norway where I described my neo-Lamarckian views on biological evolution. The following year, at the European SSE meeting in Italy, I presented a summary of Bottazzi's neglected experiments. By that time I had become convinced that those data were well worth becoming more widely known. Accordingly, I managed to publish an historical note in the *Journal of Scientific Exploration*,[1] and decided to get Bottazzi's book translated into English.

---

[1] *Journal of Scientific Exploration* 24:495–512, 2010.

In such endeavor I was fortunate to receive the assistance and cooperation of Ms. Irmeli Routti, a Finnish architect I had met forty years earlier. Her knowledge of English was definitely better than mine, as she had spent a fair share of her life in Berkeley, California, and later in different European cities. Throughout this project, she often had to struggle, with enduring patience, with the long and tortuous Italian sentences that were quite common a century ago. Luckily, they were quite comprehensible to my Italian mind, and this made our joint venture easier.

In my opinion Bottazzi's book is worth reading for a number of reasons. First and foremost, it provides one of the first instrumental records of psychokinetic (PK) events concerning simple objects like a metronome, a telegraph key, and a balance plate. Since they were hidden from the medium, Eusapia had to learn how to handle them effectively by relying on Bottazzi's instructions and on the sensory feelings of her mediumistic limbs. Most notably, some PK records certify that the two telegraph keys, separately operated by Eusapia's normal arm and mediumistic limb, were tapped simultaneously. This confirmed that the commands were coming from Eusapia's own brain/mind. These observations convinced Bottazzi that Eusapia's capacities were primarily due to her ability to temporarily generate anomalous limbs endowed with sensory and motor capacities comparable to those of normal limbs. This biological interpretation was in sharp conflict with the prevailing spiritistic view at that time.

The book is written in a rather unusual style. Every occurrence is narrated in a straightforward way, at times humorously, but never abandoning its compelling rigor. It gives the impression that each event, no matter how strange, was considered to belong to the wider realm of human experience. Likewise, the relations between Eusapia and the participants are described as growing from a somewhat formal beginning to progressively friendlier exchanges. They include screams uttered by a ticklish participant, who felt touches by mysterious hands, as well as jokes told to the spiritual entity that Eusapia considered to be her father.

Bottazzi also lists sharp objections to several categories of disbelievers ranging from those who simply had never had a chance to attend a 'séance,' to those who were stubbornly committed to their negative *a priori* attitudes. These last persons already had their own 'truth,' and strongly believed that phenomena beyond their truth could not exist. A century later things have not improved. After I finished presenting a summary of Bottazzi's experiments to the Academy of Physical and Mathematical Sciences in Naples, an influential member of the Academy could not refrain from protesting "If a student of mine had reported comparable observations, I would have kicked him in the ass!" Feeling as a faithful ambassador of other people's data,

I retorted that the remark was an unfair challenge to the group of University professors who had witnessed those experiments and had agreed with Bottazzi's conclusions. The influential member eventually offered his apologies, and I believe we are still friends.

Antonio Giuditta
Naples, May 2011

Editors' Note

The ICRL Press has as its stated purpose the publication of an assortment of specialized books related to the scholarly exploration of human consciousness. None of our efforts to date better fulfills this charter than this fascinating English translation of Professor Filippo Bottazzi's description of a sequence of impeccable experiments he designed, implemented, and oversaw over a century ago involving the celebrated medium, Eusapia Palladino. At that time Spiritualism, or Spiritism as it was known in Italy, was at its peak and had attracted the interest of many of the most notable scholars of that era, including such luminaries as Sir William Crookes, John Lord Raleigh, Sir J. J. Thompson, Sir Oliver Lodge, Frederick Myers, Marie and Pierre Curie, Charles Richet, William James, Sir Arthur Conan Doyle, and Mark Twain, among many others.

This propensity apparently had arisen in reaction to the growing materialistic character of the Industrial Revolution that tended to dismiss any spiritual dimension of human experience. Despite its rejection by the prevailing scientific establishment, spiritualism became one of the most popular and influential cultural movements of its time, prompting many significant initiatives such as the abolition of slavery, suffrage, health reforms, and improvements in labor relations. A substantial number of controlled scientific studies, like those of Bottazzi documented herein, investigated the ability of certain individuals, known as spiritual mediums, to establish contact with discarnate entities in the context of a séance, or "spirit circle," and therein to produce a variety of striking physical manifestations, such as loud raps and other noises; voices; levitations; materialized objects such as apports, spirit bodies, and body parts. Palladino was among the most celebrated of these mediums, and had already been studied extensively by many other credible investigators.

Two pertinent themes pervade Bottazzi's work. Dominant, of course, is his indisputable verification of the extraordinary abilities of this remarkable woman to display an array of anomalous physical phenomena. But also implicit in his narrative is the all-too-familiar frustration of a sincere scientific investigator to induce a modicum of professional open-mindedness in his professional colleagues of that day. Regrettably, such a suffocating burden of self-sustaining recalcitrance from contemporary academic and scientific communities continues to obstruct legitimate pursuit of understanding of this and many other valid albeit poorly understood topics. To these enduring epistemological and ideological tensions, Bottazzi's not-so-subtle scholarly vicissitudes remain pertinent indeed, and we are indebted to the translators for sharing them with us.

Robert G. Jahn
Brenda J. Dunne
April, 2011

Prof. FILIPPO BOTTAZZI

Direttore dell'Istituto di Fisiologia Sperimentale
della R. Università di Napoli

FENOMENI

MEDIANICI

osservati in una serie di sedute

fatte con Eusapia Paladino

NAPOLI

FRANCESCO PERRELLA, EDITORE

1909

To the Reader

Considering the relevance of experimental investigations of 'mediumistic phenomena,' I have accepted the invitation by the well-known editor Mr. Perrella to publish in book form the account of results which my colleagues and I have obtained in a series of 'mediumistic sessions' with E. Palladino about two years ago.

This report differs from the one I published in *Rivista d'Italia*, not only for some text changes and corrections, but also because the report of the seventh session summarily published in that journal is here complete, and the report of a further session, the eighth, is now added with new figures.

Additions could be more numerous since I participated in other sessions after those whose results are reported here. But what aim would they serve? Results were always qualitatively the same. So, it makes no difference to report those of thirty sessions rather than those of ten sessions. What really matters is that they took place under the best conditions apt to eliminate the possibility of fraud by the *medium*, or to detect it whenever the *medium* may resort to it.

Hence, I will only mention that the last observations have confirmed my conviction of the real occurrence of mediumistic phenomena.

It is necessary to continue searching, limiting our search to one or two events in order to determine all the conditions producing them. It is useful and soon will become necessary to make experiments with other *mediums*, possibly with *mediums* who have not yet made money with their mediumistic capacities, and who may be young and disciplined.

I believe Eusapia Palladino is now at her last trials. She is old, weak, and ill. Her mediumistic power is progressively weakening, as I realized by comparing her last sessions with those of two years ago.

Mediums exist in larger numbers than one may believe. But the best ones are afraid to expose themselves and make public their exceptional capacities. We need to look for them and to convince them that our intentions are serious, and that experiments based on scientific methods are necessary.

Naples, January 1909.

F.B.

I. **Introduction.**

Additional experiments, new mediumistic sessions with Eusapia Palladino? Yes, and this is how I was prompted to start them.

Before reading Barzini's articles on *Corriere della Sera* I was perhaps a disbeliever or rather indifferent in regard to mediumistic phenomena. I had read little or nothing of them and had never attended 'spiritu-alistic' sessions. I had heard of those held by Richet and of others which had taken place in Rome and had been attended by very esteemed friends. Also because one of them asserted that Palladino is almost always resorting to fraud, I was more inclined to deny the existence of these phenomena than to accept it. I might even have made a statement that I didn't think it worthwhile for a scientist or a naturalist to attend spiritualist sessions.

This is not surprising if one considers that the vast majority of people who have not attended a medium-istic session with Eusapia Palladino share such an attitude. Indeed, someone I hold in high esteem in Naples replied with a disdainful refusal even today to my cordial suggestion to participate in at least one session.

But Barzini's articles, which I read carefully, impressed me, and I switched from disbelief or indif-ference to doubt and then to the wish to look into the matter myself.

One evening having heard from Nicola Minutillo, a lawyer, that he had met Palladino and had attended several sessions, I asked him keenly to let me participate in one of them as soon as he could arrange it. But nothing followed.

Later on, my young friend from Turin, Dr. Carlo Foà, assistant professor in the physiology laboratory of that city, sent me and Professor Gino Galeotti, my colleague in this university, three issues of the newspaper *La Stampa*. They reported an accurate account of the phenomena observed by him and Doctors A. Herlitzka and A. Agazzotti, together with other gentlemen from Turin, in three sessions Palladino granted them after those in Genoa. Having eagerly read those articles, Galeotti and I looked at each other very impressed and with the same thought. Identical words came simultaneously to our lips:

"We want to see these events; we want to touch them with our own hands and with no delay! We need to get hold of Palladino, to know when she will come back to Naples, and induce her to grant us some sessions as well... here, in this laboratory where we investigate the phenomena of life every day with the detachment of those who hold the discovery of scientific truth as their sole objective and have made experimental investigation the utmost goal of their existence. Here, in this quiet environment free of all passions it will become unnecessary to seal doors, inspect rooms to avoid deceits, ask ladies to undress Palladino and examine her 'venerable' body, as Barzini likes to say."

And by exciting and elating each other, as it happens when the idea of a nice experiment on a dog or rabbit flashes through the mind of a professional experimentalist (apologies are due to poor Eusapia for the comparison that may appear irreverent only to profane people), we added:

"We need to record everything graphically and photographically ... all what may be recordable ... Will she be able to affect photographic plates? ... Will she light up a screen of barium platinum-cyanide? ... Will she discharge a golden leaf electroscope without touching it? ..." and so we kept going on, letting our fantasy fly but having always in mind the need for the most rigorous scientific methodology.

"How wonderful were the descriptions by Barzini, but what about the documentation? What about the evidence? ... Yes, several people witnessed them ... but several people had already witnessed before and yet the doubt still lingers. One needs to provide documents similar to those of our scientific publications."

What would my colleagues in physiology in Italy and abroad say if I were to publish a series of observations on, let's say, nerve excitability, muscle contraction, effects of stimulation of a nerve center, etc., lacking information on the nature and intensity of the stimuli we used, lacking photographic records of the electric changes on the nerve, of faithful graphic reproductions of the shape, height, width, duration, etc. of the muscle contractions?

Well, we needed to obtain similar records of at least some of the phenomena Palladino is capable of producing by her mediumistic power. When they will be in our hands, having made it impossible (as much as possible) for Palladino to produce the phenomena by using her hands, feet, in brief her body, then doubting people will believe or they will rush to start personal investigations. Disbelievers will have second thoughts and indifferent people will be impressed and will no longer despise the most marvelous phenomena yet offered to scientific research.

*****

But two difficulties needed to be overcome: getting Palladino's approval and choosing participants in the experiments. To overcome the first difficulty, I quickly thought of obtaining a letter of recommendation to Eusapia by Prof. Charles Richet. The letter worked like a charm: Eusapia spread it out, cast a quick look with her very swift eye to the lower left corner where there was a certain conventional sign, and she returned the letter to me straight away. I said: "But this is for you." She answered: "Keep it, is OK with me." And she didn't need anything else. Having become docile, meek, and agreeable, she approved of all our wishes.

When she later convinced herself from some talks luckily made by Galeotti that he knew Prof. Cesare Lombroso and his daughters and grandchildren, her docility and mere gentleness, her cold kindness with which she had accepted us, gave way to vivid gaiety, true joy to be among people who, as she phrased it "could demonstrate to have close ties with Carlo Richet and Cesare Lombroso." I believe they were people whom Eusapia most worshipped in the world, thinking of them as two deities.

So, within a few minutes we became friends. We decided how many sessions were to be held, and she left us free to choose the other participants, only asking to include her acquaintance Prof. T. De Amicis, in fact showing a keen desire to include him. The date for the first session was set.

As to the persons to be selected, we thought they should all be newcomers to mediumistic sessions, except the one designated by Palladino. They should all be of undisputed scientific authority and lacking the vanity to make untimely communication with the so-called political press. In so doing we did not mean to hide our experiment in mystery for fear of damaging our reputation as 'university professors,' but only because every serious experimenter has the habit of not publishing his results while the experiment is still going on, that is until it is completed and subjected to all possible criticism. We were well aware of Leonardo's sentence that "the world is full of infinite reasons that were never investigated" and of the truism that all phenomena are worth becoming the subject of scientific investigation. Being almost convinced that the so-called mediumistic phenomena are natural phenomena whose determinism is still beyond our reach, we meant to carry out these experiments only to demonstrate their reality to ourselves, and possibly to others too, and in the hope of clarifying their nature to at least some degree.

After several attempts and long discussions, the Observation Committee for the first six sessions included:

Dr. Gino Galeotti, full professor of general pathology in the Royal University of Naples;

Dr. Tommaso De Amicis, full professor of dermatology and syphilography in the same University;

Dr. Oscar Scarpa, free docent of physics and professor in charge of electro-chemistry in the Royal Superior Polytechnic School of Naples;

Engineer Luigi Lombardi, full professor of electrotechnology and in charge of technical physics in the same School;

Dr. Sergio Pansini, recently nominated full professor of medical semiotics in the Royal University of Naples;

and I, the undersigned.

The Committee did not remain the same in all the sessions. For reasons beyond his control Prof. Lombardi could participate in only the first and sixth sessions and was replaced in the other sessions by engineer Emanuele Jona, director of electrical services of the Pirelli and C. company in Milan, and president of the Italian Electrotechnical Association. When the venerable senator Antonio Cardarelli, professor of clinical medicine in this Royal University, heard of the results obtained in the first three sessions, he expressed his wish to participate in the following sessions. And all of us, Palladino included, felt flattered to have such an honorable man as a collaborator.

Two sessions[2] were also attended by Mrs. Bottazzi, following a special request by Eusapia, and three other sessions were attended by the lawyer Nicola Minutillo, an independent lecturer of Roman Law in this University. We warmly thank him for having offered us the possibility to meet Palladino, and to obtain her address in Naples, which we did not know.

Of the persons mentioned, four participated in all six sessions: I, Galeotti, Scarpa, and Pansini. Lombardi attended the first and sixth sessions; Minutillo the first two and the sixth; Cardarelli the last three; Jona the second, fourth, and fifth; Mrs. Bottazzi the second and third; and De Amicis all but the second.

---

[2]Bottazzi is referring to the six mediumistic sessions initially planned [note by the translator, AG].

Apart from these participants, no other person was present in the entire laboratory, except the technical mechanic Luigi Saggiomo, who stayed away from the experiment room, and at times one assistant of mine, Doctor Giuseppe Buglia, who was studying in his room. Nonetheless, despite their being far from our room and from the recording apparatus room, they heard several times the blows which invisible hands produced on the séance table, the loud downfall of the table lifted to considerable heights,... and the screams made by Doctor Pansini who could not avoid uttering them every time mysterious fingers touched his arm or tickled his armpit. The latter events greatly amused us. They could not be suppressed despite my serving as a watchdog during the sessions, mumbling against anyone's laughs, shouts, or talk, chastising Pansini and asking him to exert all his inhibitory powers.

II. The Place Where the Experiments Were Made.

My keenest desire was that the experiments would be made not in a private house, but in a scientific laboratory. There we interrogate nature open-mindedly, prompted only by the desire to know the truth, and we attentively follow the unwrapping of this and that natural event, be it in the order of physics, chemistry, or physiology. A private house, although respectable people and acquaintances may dwell in it, is not the right environment for serious research. Too many people usually remain outside the room where the party of observers gathers around the *medium*. It is difficult or impossible to transport the required instruments, especially if they are to be taken away every evening. It is impossible to arrange them in the most suitable way to allow the automatic recording of the phenomena without the *medium* noticing it.

But Eusapia's reluctance to enter laboratories and consent to scientific experiments dealing with her mediumistic capacities, declared by some, was against my desire. In fact, she started to propose that the sessions take place in the house of the lawyer N. Minutillo, which she had already visited, or in my house. I pointed out that my house was far from the city, and that we had not known Prof. Minutillo long enough to ask his apartment to be put at our disposal. Later on, without showing much interest, and expressing it casually as a mere possibility, I said to her: "Why not get together in my laboratory? I have a small room there which looks like it is made for such a purpose. It is far from the street, surrounded by laboratory rooms on three sides and by an interior garden on the fourth. The environment is calm, solitary, not a soul in sight at night, and inside only people of our choice. It is the only place where we can meet without anyone getting wind of it. No doormen or servants will be spying on us, and journalists will not be hunting for news to be printed the next day in local papers."

Due to Palladino's antipathy for journalists and for articles in political newspapers dealing with her,[3] this last argument won over her reluctance. So, having finally been convinced that she would not see dogs or rabbits on vivisection tables (anyway, how could this be possible in the middle of the night?), and that her consent would also very much please Prof. Richet, she accepted my proposal and the date for the first session was set.

Our little experiment room is one of the farthest rooms in the Laboratory of experimental physiology of this University in Sant'Andrea delle Dame and is part of the section exclusively used as my personal laboratory. The section comprises two parallel sets of rooms. One set, the outer one, looks out on Costantinopoli Street, while the other set, the inner one, overlooks the inner Laboratory garden. The first set consists

---

[3]She complained to me about Barzini's articles in *Corriere della Sera*, which were actually very nice and kind, and in particular about her picture printed on the cover of the booklet in which the articles were collected.

of three rooms, the second of four. The small room where experiments were made is the second of the inner set. A room used for chemical analyses precedes it, and another room harboring a galvanometer and a Lippmann's capillary electrometer follows it. The room which adjoins it on the outer side is used for polarimetric and spectrophotometric analyses. The experiment room has three doors, two aligned in the same direction, one leading to the galvanometer's room, always locked from the inside with a key, while through the other one our party entered the experiment room. The third door, also locked with a key, provides access to the polarimetric and spectrophotometric room of the outer set. This door formed the back of the mediumistic cabinet, as shown in one of the photographs included here. The mediumistic cabinet was set in the wide opening of the thick wall leading to the locked door. It was closed in front by two curtains of black fabric hung from an iron rod, and sliding on it by rings. These were kindly provided by Eusapia.

In the experiment room there were the following pieces of furniture: first of all, the séance table and seven or eight chairs around it to be used by those who participated in the session. On the left hand side,[4] there was one bookcase with three shelves made of fir and painted gray, on which we placed many objects used in our experiments. Farther to the left, against the wall on the entrance side of the room, there was a

---

[4]Left and right sides are always indicated in respect to the person sitting at the séance table and facing the mediumistic cabinet.

couch covered by fabric made of horsehair and in front of it a small carved walnut table holding paper and pencils for those who might wish to write notes and comments during the session or in the intervals. On the wall opposite of the mediumistic cabinet there was a low window opening to the garden. Its glass windows and shutters were always tightly closed. Close to the window there was a decimal balance on the floor. It was intended to weigh Palladino's body before and after each session, but was used only to weigh table and chairs moved or lifted by the *medium*. Farther to the right, opposite to the cabinet, there was a slate shelf on the wall. In the corner between this wall and the adjacent right wall, there was a Serino water pipe with brass faucet and a marble basin beneath. Apart from the furniture and various scientific instruments close to the walls, the room did not contain anything else, being relatively small, as mentioned.

Four electric incandescent lamps were in the room, two placed on movable supports and two fixed on top of the door frame facing the entrance door. One of the movable lamps was covered by a colorless glass (lamp 1), while the other lamp was painted red with many color layers, and was the least bright lamp (lamp 4). Both of them were placed on the slate shelf or on the balance plate, depending on whether it was decided to give more or less light to the séance table or to Palladino's body. The red color of the two fixed lamps (lamp 2 and lamp 3) was to provide intermediate degrees of brightness between those of lamps 1 and 4. Obviously, lamp 1 was lit only for a few minutes at the beginning of the session until the séance table would order: "less light!" using its conventional language of beats or blows on the floor. Soon thereafter lamps 2 and 3 were turned off according to requests for less light. Only very rarely was the experiment conducted in darkness; almost always at least lamp 4 remained lit, which allowed a faint light to come from the above right on the table and the sitters almost below. This light was sufficient to see Palladino s hands and body clearly from her waist up, and to allow definite identification of our faces without effort, and even to read the time on the dials of our clocks. Nevertheless, from the fourth session on, to avoid total darkness and still not refusing to obey her request for lower light than that provided by lamp number 4, I had a rheostat inserted in the electrical circuit of the latter lamp. The rheostat was fastened on the wall at hand's reach to allow further lowering of the light without the need to turn it off. The switches of the four lamps were hung on the backs of four chairs by long cords, or they were left within the reach of four participants.

The arrangement of the furniture was never substantially changed in the room throughout all the sessions. What was always changed from session to session was the nature and position of the objects placed in the mediumistic cabinet. These variations will be minutely described each time.

III. Nature of the Experiments and Experimental Arrangements.

In the majority of previous experiments with Eusapia Palladino, observers were sufficiently satisfied to witness levitation and movement of furniture or other objects, to be touched and pulled by invisible hands, to witness apparitions of hands, heads, and bodies, or *materializations*, and to describe tactile or visible sensations. On the other hand, however trustworthy these people were or are, and accustomed to strict scientific observation, however universally highly esteemed names they have in the scientific world, like those of Cesare Lombroso, Carlo Richet, Camillo Flammarion and many others, no one can doubt the fact that much superior to a simple description of sensations felt is the automatic graphic recording of phenomena taking place at mediumistic sessions, or at least of those phenomena that can be registered graphically or photographically.

Contemporary experimental science has found invaluable help in methods of graphic recording because they replace the simple description of natural phenomena with an automatic documentation. The advantage that follows is twofold. It is not only a question of substituting personal appreciation of the phenomena with automatic recording, already a relevant thing as such. Undoubtedly, it is one thing to say: "Mr. X present at a given session heard at a certain moment the tapping of a telegraph key in the mediumistic cabinet while the *medium* did not touch it with her visible hands." But it is a different thing to present to an incredulous public a graphic tracing of the modified electromagnetic signals coming from the key and written on a sheet of blackened paper placed far away from the *medium*. Indeed, it is customary to say that Mr. X could have been victim of auditory hallucination. Nor is it worth adding that everybody present heard the tapping of the key. The stubborn disbelievers will answer: "That's fine, but it could have been a collective hallucination by all those who were more or less in the same attentive state of mind, expecting the phenomenon to happen. Or it could have been somebody else, not seen by you, whose presence you would not have suspected in the adjoining room, upstairs or downstairs in the house, who knocked or hammered a nail in the wall, etc." What could you answer to such objections? Always the same reply: "I heard it clearly, I have no doubt in my mind that the key was tapped." All this only amounts to personal assertion of sensory perceptions under conditions that are really not optimal with respect to the tranquility and serenity of mind. Thus, there can be no doubt that whenever it is possible to arrange conditions in such a way that mediumistic phenomena may leave an indelible trace, this method should not be neglected. This would put an end to either exaltations due to the excessive credibility of some, or to doubts and skepticism by others. Undoubtedly, there will always be disbelievers, but they will not be people whose judgment we value much. They will no longer be scientists who understand the value and significance of graphic automatic recording of natural phenomena. I hope scientists will yield to the evidence of the facts I am going to present and document. The stubborn disbelievers, the irreducible disbelievers, will be and remain ignorant people lacking scientific training who do not appreciate the validity of our methods of investigation. Among them will be those who are unable to understand for lack of a naturalistic education. They have a primitive manner of thinking, and when facing the truth that it is not the sun that circles around the earth but the opposite, they say: "Maybe, but I see the sun circling, not the earth."

Science should not worry about these people, for however numerous, they do not slow down its progress. Science, in its great advancement, leaves them behind, not paying attention to them.

I mentioned that the method of graphic recording has an additional merit. The description we can provide of phenomena, even of those occurring under our eyes and in full light, is always fragmentary, partial, and inevitably incomplete. Only an instrumental automatic recording can tell us precisely how long a phenomenon has lasted; *how* it developed; whether it was continuous or not; whether there were variations in intensity and at what time; and what other events were associated with it, maybe in synchrony.

The report I will be making of the phenomena taking place during our sixth session will demonstrate, for example, that not all participants agreed over some facts; some of them affirming, some denying that a certain phenomenon occurred. But an inexorable physical device had recorded the phenomenon, and the following day everybody looked at the trace and did agree upon this particular fact.

The observations made by Flammarion and by Barzini are quite beautiful and well described, but where are the documents? To believe, we must rely on the literal description they provide. We must trust not only them, who on their honor say that they are telling the truth — which nobody doubts — but their sensations as well. Leonardo wrote that there is nothing more deceiving than our senses. The main value of present methods of investigation of natural phenomena is based, whenever possible, on the principle of replacing the sole testimony of senses by the automatic recording of the phenomena.

It was only recently that our friends Drs. A. Herlitzka, C. Foà, and A. Agazzotti, assistants in the Laboratory of Physiology in Turin, obtained graphic records of some phenomena produced psychically by Palladino. But in the report of their sessions that they prepared for the newspaper La Stampa (issues of March 1, March 4, and March 6, 1907), they did not include the traces they obtained, nor have we been able to see them.

We succeeded in obtaining several traces, which will be published in this book. To be more precise, we will present photographs of the original traces, which I jealously guard in the archive of my laboratory.

I will mention in detail how these traces were obtained, case by case. Here I will only describe methods and procedures devised to obtain such traces, while the *medium* was not aware of our doing so.

Two essential parts are to be distinguished in every graphic recording. One consists of the receiving instruments, those on which forces or actions are directly exerted when they are to be recorded. The other part consists of the actual recording devices, including the surface on which the recording is made, to preserve the traces of actions occurring at a distance. Actually, this is the method of indirect recording, the only one feasible in our case. I will explain it with an example.

Consider a metal cylinder covered with a sheet of white paper blackened by smoke. The cylinder continuously turns around its axis at constant speed, be it faster or slower. The tip of a pen rests on the cylinder and at its other end is fastened to a support. The pen can move vertically on a horizontal axis. When moving, the point draws a curved line, an arc of a circle whose center is the axis around which the pen rotates. By means of a counterweight, the pen rests in a horizontal position when idle. Consider furthermore that a telegraph key is placed on a table with its button connected to the pen by a cotton or silk thread. When the *medium* is told: "Press on the key button without touching it with your visible hand, but using your mediumistic power," the *medium* lowers it and people hear the tapping of the metal tip of the key on the metal block below. But at the same time the lowered button of the key pulls down the pen by its attached thread, and its point draws a white line on the blackened surface of the paper.

If we observed the button go down, we had a visual sensation, and if we heard the tap we had an acoustic sensation. But these sensations appear and remain within us. They diminish, vanish, and leave no trace except in our memory. But to these sensations and to the key movement, we now have the corresponding white line drawn by the pen on the blackened paper. If the blackened paper is later fixed with any varnish, the mark or line can no longer be cancelled. You may take a photograph and reproduce it, while keeping the original.

The above method is known as *direct recording*, as the moving body directly pulls the pen and makes it draw a line. One may also use an indirect method.

Instead of the pen just described, let us place on the cylinder another pen which may be pulled by an iron block whenever the block happens to be magnetized by an electric current going through an insulated cord wrapped around the block. Let us also insert the telegraph key into this electric circuit so that when the key button is up the electric circuit remains open, but when the key is pressed down and hits the metal block below, the circuit is closed. Thus, with every depression of the key button there will be a closure of the electric circuit, and an opening with every later spontaneous uplift. At the same time, at each closing and opening there will be respectively a pulling and a release of the metal pen which obeys the electromagnetic signal. This will produce two white short lines, one going down and the other going up, which will remain distinct and will not overlap if the blackened cylinder keeps rotating. This is the method of *indirect recording*, based on the use of electricity.

If the force is applied instead to a hermetically sealed air-filled metal drum, one surface of which consists of a rubber leaf, and this drum is connected to a similar drum equipped with a recording pen and connected to it by a rubber tube of any desired length, every pressure on the rubber leaf of the first drum, or *receptor drum*, compresses the inside air and produces a rising of the elastic surface of the *recording drum*. Since a pen is connected with such surface, the rising pen will draw an upward curved line. Conversely, when the pen goes down due to the decreased pressure on the receptive membrane, it will draw a white line on the paper that will go in the opposite direction. This is indirect recording done by means of the air present in the closed system of the two drums connected by a rubber tube. But the system may also be filled with liquid, or partly air and partly liquid (water and mercury, etc.). On the liquid filling a U-shaped glass tube, one can put a floating device equipped with a pen writing on the usual cylinder. The device will be placed on one of the two U-arms, while the other arm is connected with a long airtight transmitter tube. When one presses the elastic membrane of the drum, the compressed air lowers the mercury in the *manometer* arm connected with the rubber tube, and makes the mercury rise to the same extent in the arm harboring the floating device. The floating device and connecting pen are also lifted, making the point of the pen draw an upward white line on the blackened paper and later on another downward white line when the float goes back down.

We have used these and similar methods to record some of the mediumistic phenomena produced by Palladino. Receiving instruments were placed in the mediumistic cabinet, and arranged as I will describe later. Palladino never knew anything of this. She was usually uninterested in examining the interior of the cabinet, which was always covered by curtains when experimenters and *medium* entered the room. Indeed, if invited to look at it, she sharply refused, saying it was of no concern to her.

Recording instruments were instead in the adjoining room, which as previously mentioned, was used for spectrophotometric analyses, etc. They were situated on a solid wood table by the door that formed the back wall of the cabinet, but naturally on the other side and in the arrangement shown in Fig. 1, page 52.

The receiving instruments were connected to the recorders by electric cords and rubber tubes going partly through the keyhole, partly through other holes made in the hermetically closed door.

On each session day, having already agreed on the evening experiments, most frequently with Professors Galeotti and Scarpa, I carefully arranged all instruments in their place in either room together with the technical mechanic of the laboratory. Then, my collaborator Dr. Gennaro d'Errico took a photograph of the mediumistic cabinet whose curtains had been moved laterally and of the recording instruments on the table. This having been done, all doors and windows were closed. The experiment room was to be opened again only upon arrival of Eusapia, and the room with the recording instruments only upon the end of the session, to obtain a first and quick view of the results obtained. After that the two rooms were locked again, to be reopened only the day after on my return to the laboratory. At this time, Dr. d'Errico took a new photograph of the mediumistic cabinet. By looking at the two photographs taken the day before and the day after the session, with all the objects, instruments, mediumistic table, etc. left in the same place where they were when we left the room, everyone could observe, as if he had been present at the session, all movements, transfers, overturning of chairs and objects, everything that the mediumistic power of Palladino had produced during each session (except the first one).

The time curve was then added below the recorded traces on cylinders by setting the cylinders in motion with the same speed they had rotated the evening before. For the benefit of those not familiar with physiological methods, I will note that this was easily accomplished, as we used nearly always a Straub-Heder electric kymograph set in motion by two big accumulators. Since the charge of the accumulators and the resistance of the rheostat placed in between the accumulators and the electric motor were constant, the rotation speed of the two cylinders placed one on top of the other around the same axis had to be the same every time they were set in motion. In the last sessions we decided to use the electric kymograph exclusively, and to place the switch closing the electric circuit of the cylinders' motor in the experiment room.

One reason was to prevent cylinders from rotating needlessly before mediumistic phenomena started to appear. Another reason was to avoid somebody in the adjacent room having to set the kymograph in motion when he heard the command coming from the experiment room. This person would have been the technical mechanic of the physiology laboratory, a most loyal person to be absolutely trusted. We were taught these expedients by some inconveniences that occurred in the first sessions, and by having once used, in addition to the electric kymograph, some clockwork kymographs. As the charge of these instruments lasts only a short period of time, they need to be set in motion and stopped only at desired moments. In the photographs of the mediumistic cabinet taken during the last sessions one can see this switch fixed on the interior frame of the cabinet, which could be reached by hand by any nearby participant. At a given moment, as soon as the phenomena to be recorded started to be produced, the switch was turned on and soon thereafter in the silence of the night one could hear the faint buzzing of the started electric motor in the adjacent room. From that moment on the kymograph remained in motion until the session ended. Obviously, the six writing pens traced horizontal white lines until they were activated, and on those white lines they recorded their movements when the receiving instruments were put into action. As later detailed, of the six pens, four relied on electromagnetic signals, the fifth one relied on signals coming from a Marey tambour, and the sixth one relied on signals from a François-Frank mercury manometer. These traces were then fixed according to our usual routine, and they were carefully studied by me and Professors Galeotti and Scarpa. As I said, they are now jealously guarded by me.

I wrote a detailed report of the phenomena taking place during each session, sometimes on the same night, otherwise on the following morning. By going back to these reports, and agreeing with my friends upon some dubious or controversial points, I am now able to write this account with clear and relaxed mind.

During sessions it was impossible to take notes, given the rapidity with which phenomena often unfolded. Their manifestation was so irregular and unpredictable, so totally independent from any will and norm that in order not to miss a single event, which might perhaps turn out to be the most important of the whole evening, your mind had to be constantly highly alert and attention always aroused. Whoever observed these events, especially if he was also guarding the *medium*, definitely could not divert his attention and interrupt his observation to write even short notes. And whoever writes cannot diligently observe. In fact, any observer's thoughts had to be translated automatically into graphic marks, since dictating also disturbed observer and *medium*. As a result, session reports needed to be written afterwards, trusting one's own memory and the testimony of participants.

But memory of the phenomena observed during mediumistic sessions has always remained so clear and lucid to me (I cannot speak for other people) that the next morning, when writing my report, I felt like I was again participating in the session. This happens with all phenomena of great interest which are strongly sculpted in us. And I should add that, at least for me, there was almost no interruption between the end of the session and the moment I started to write down my report. After attending a session with Palladino, you do not sleep at night. And if you sleep, you experience such vivid dreams that the whole sequence of observed events starts again in your mind with almost cinematographic precision. In fact, in such a half-sleep state memories become layered, reassembled, rearranged. And I later found that my pen was slow in following the progression of my thoughts, as the memory of experienced sensations was so persistent. At times, to facilitate my reporting task, I found it useful rather to go back to the experiment room in the morning, and close myself inside it to live again, while noting and writing, those unforgettable hours.

In any case, not everything that was seen, heard, or felt by everybody is reproduced here, nor is the rigorous sequence of events maintained. What purpose would it serve? Many details of secondary importance are neglected, many observations made several times are described only once, many feelings experienced by others are only briefly mentioned. I concentrate only on matters of major relevance, mainly on phenomena assessed by all participants and discussed at that moment, or on those which were graphically recorded.

IV. **The Séance Table and the Mediumistic Cabinet.**

Since the black curtains were kindly provided by Eusapia, I only had to have the séance table made. It was 0.95 m long, 0.48 m wide, and 0.78 m high, made of polished fir, but neither painted nor varnished, and weighed 6.2 kg.

The dimensions of the mediumistic cabinet were:

width	1.20 m
depth (from curtains to back door)	0.90 m
height (from the floor to the curtains' top)	2.50 m

But the curtains were a little bit longer, so they not only touched the floor but folded up on it by about ten centimeters. "This is indispensable," said Eusapia to me, but I do not know why.

The distance from the closed curtains to the center of the séance table was 1.40 m. Everybody could easily check the position of the table with his foot during the session. Scarpa, having placed the table at the distance indicated by Eusapia, had an iron rod inserted into the floor corresponding to the centre of the table. It is worth pointing out right away that just a few minutes after the beginning of the session the séance table started to move. This was also due to the fact that as phenomena intensified, levitations and rappings taking place outside the cabinet were followed by movements occurring inside the cabinet. Palladino showed an irresistible tendency to get closer to the curtains, dragging with her the séance table and along with it the whole mediumistic chain.

Although she approached and at times felt the need to touch the curtains, *she never put her hand inside the cabinet nor did she ever inspect it before or during sessions.* When she was so close to the curtain that she could have reached the objects placed inside the cabinet in the foreground with her visible hands, she would have needed to bend her trunk backwards and extend her arms to the utmost degree in the same direction, something none of us ever saw her doing. But even if she had tried to do so, the hands of two guardians on her right and left *never abandoned the hands of the medium*, and would have felt the contact with these objects, a thing that never occurred.

New experimental arrangements were very often made inside the mediumistic cabinet. Usually, people arranged it to contain a few small tables and stools, chairs and variable number of objects: a mandolin or a guitar, a water bottle with glasses, etc. All these objects were placed so that they could be moved, transported, or thrown at a distance. Trying not to be too innovative, knowing that Palladino disliked changes, we put in the cabinet some of the usual toys (trumpet, brush, pen, mandolin, etc.). Above all, she disliked substituting a known person with a new one in the mediumistic chain but also merely, for example,

placing a plate of soft clay for mediumistic imprints on
the small table or on the floor rather than on a chair,
the way she liked it. Starting from the second session,
the receiving instruments which she was supposed to
activate and the board supporting them most of the
time, were fastened and immobilized in such a way
that Palladino almost never succeeded in moving them,
whatever force she used. She became visibly irritated
at this, and more than once she clearly expressed it
during the sessions, although outside of them Eusapia
did not even hint at them. To us this was of major
importance. When, after the first movements of the
table and curtains, invisible limbs of the *medium* penetrated into the mediumistic cabinet containing a table
or a chair, the first thing they did, strangely enough,
was usually not to touch or move the objects placed
on them, however light or heavy they were, but to lift,
push, or drag the table or the chair. Understandably,
objects we had carefully placed there would be overturned or fall on the floor. If there were electric cords,
elastic tubes, etc., they would get tangled and possibly
broken. Therefore, I had to immobilize not only the
support (the little table or the wooden board, etc.) but
also the instruments on top. Electric cords and tubes
were led through holes pierced in the wooden board,
minimizing their length on the board surface. I had
noticed the first evening that the *medium* had been
able to move, lift, and put in oblique position a table

wedged in the mediumistic cabinet and weighing 21.9 kg. So, all objects in the mediumistic cabinet had to be immobilized with iron bars, or with wooden bars fixed on the wall or to the back door, even if this limited the number of observable phenomena, as our objective was to observe those which were most important to us.

Indeed, this is the first step in scientific investigation of mediumistic phenomena. Up to now, Palladino had been left free to throw out anything, play the mandolin, carry away water bottles and glasses, overturn and lift all kinds of objects. We started to put some brakes on her inexhaustible mediumistic activity, and forced her to do things she had never done before. We limited the extent of her mediumistic manifestations to pinpoint at least some of the essential conditions required to let her produce the phenomena.

I am convinced that for Palladino it was easier to drag a heavy table outside the cabinet, or lift a chair from the mediumistic cabinet to the séance table, than to press an electric key or move the rod of a metronome, all this with her invisible hands. I will get back to these considerations, but for now I will say that undoubtedly this depended on the fact that these movements of skill, rather than force, were new to her, or at least unfamiliar. That is to say that to do delicate movements, the invisible hands of Eusapia needed the same kind of education and exercise as her visible hands. Without them, even visible hands may well be capable of rough and violent movements, but not of acts requiring finesse and skill.

I had better stop now, not to turn upside down the order of my report where conclusions and general considerations are to be logically found in the last pages.

Let me then start reporting our observations without further ado.

V. First Session (April 17, 1907).

At 21:00, barometric pressure = 760.79, temperature = 9.7°C.

Present were Professors De Amicis, Lombardi, Galeotti, Scarpa, Pansini, and me, and the lawyer Minutillo. The session started at 21:22.

We formed the chain around the séance table. Guarding hands, feet, and knees of the *medium* were at first Bottazzi and Lombardi, the first one on the right and the second on the left. Then the same persons continued, but changing positions according to Eusapia's wish.

Half an hour passed, but no important phenomena took place except the usual creaks, blows, and bends and mediocre levitations of the table.

We tried another pair of guards, since in the mediumistic chain the two persons connected to the *medium* seem to be most effective in the mysterious collaboration that constitutes the very reason of the chain, and is consistently required by the *medium*. We tried Bottazzi and Scarpa, then Scarpa and Galeotti, finally Galeotti and Pansini.

Eusapia made painful efforts, became restless, and said every now and then that the environment was not favorable, that she felt something unfriendly in the mediumistic environment. And she might not have been wrong. Rarely had there been an assembly around her with such unprejudiced minds, rigorous and attentive, with more objective people ready to pass a judgment as well as it is humanly possible over the reality or illusion of the expected phenomena, and ready to say in all fairness: "They are natural phenomena," or: "They are tricks and illusions of senses."

Upon Palladino's request, the session was interrupted for a few minutes.

Having re-established the chain, with Scarpa guarding Palladino's left limbs, he felt touched on his right hip and was aware of a blow of fresh air coming from the cabinet, accompanied by a slight movement of the curtain.

Finally the pair Galeotti-Pansini assumed custody of the *medium*, and soon we started hearing movements in the cabinet.

But let us see what we had placed there.

A table weighing 21.900 kg with two shelves filling all the space in the cabinet, and at a distance of about 20 cm from the curtain.

On the top level:

a) a cylinder covered with paper blackened by smoke, free to turn around its vertical axis and upheld by a metal frame, with a pen attached and its point touching the paper. If the cylinder had been rotated, the pen would have drawn a horizontal line;

b) a letter-weighing balance carrying a horizontal pen fixed on the support of the plate with its point on the cylinder, but at some distance from the other one.

If the balance-plate had been pressed lowering the pen, the point would have registered a vertical line;

c) a partly charged Zimmermann electric metronome connected with a Desprez signal placed in the adjacent room. Its electric contact is established by a platinum point which at every full swing of the rod plunges into a well of mercury;

d) a telegraph key connected to another Desprez signal;

e) a pear-shaped elastic rubber connected by means of a long, hard-walled rubber tube to a François-Frank mercury manometer placed in the adjacent room;

f) a hen feather;

g) a small cardboard box tied with several turns of a metal wire and containing visiting cards and a couple of lenses.

On the bottom level:

h) a big terracotta plate containing a 2-cm-thick layer of soft clay mixed with glycerin and water;

i) a mandolin;

j) a small drum with two sticks;

k) a tin trumpet.

All these instruments were simply left on the table, not fastened to the boards.

Given the little relevance of the phenomena observed during the first session, the sequence of their appearance is not worth describing. I will summarize in a few words the results obtained.

The heavy table in the cabinet was violently shaken several times with visible efforts by the *medium*, who used her arms and legs to this purpose. At times and in spurts the table was dragged out of the cabinet from its front left corner, corresponding to the right side of Palladino, and lifted in such a way that after the session it was found tilted backwards and to the right by about 10° with respect to the floor. Naturally, all objects on the table were moved or upturned. Only the cylinder and the balance had retained their original positions. The traces on the smoked paper told us that the cylinder had rotated from left to right, counter-clockwise, and the pen of the letter-weighing balance had written very irregular marks corresponding to the blows of the metal block on the support of the balance that we heard when the table was moving. But movements of cylinder and balance were undoubtedly due to shocks and movements of the table. In fact, having put the table back to its original position and then moving it step by step to where we found it, I could artificially reproduce the trace on the cylinder, which for this reason is of no value.

The metronome was also set in motion. We clearly heard the tic-tac of its swing for which there is a corresponding trace of the Desprez signal on the cylinder in the adjacent room. But the rod of the metronome was also undoubtedly shaken and forced to oscillate by the violent movements of the table, as I verified by reproducing this phenomenon artificially.

The mandolin was found on the floor where it had fallen, surely because of the tilting of the table.

On the other hand, the cardboard box was certainly thrown to the floor, as we heard it falling at a time the table was not shaken. Furthermore, the box was found on the same side the table had been lifted, not on the opposite side. In any case, it was not flung open.

Thus, the session brought very poor results, the poorest of all. But connoisseurs say that first sessions always go like this, due to the lack of familiarity between the *medium* and the members of the chain. Yet, how many 'smart or clever guys' have judged mediumistic phenomena by sessions like this one!

How definitely peculiar is this need of agreement, tuning, homogeneity among participants to a mediumistic session to allow the phenomena to manifest. The need is affirmed by everybody, but that makes it no less mysterious and unexplainable.

Certainly, the first evening Eusapia found herself ill at ease with us. She seemed inhibited by the vigilant expectation of most of us, and Scarpa's inquisitive look was evidently not compensated by De Amicis' and Minutillo's kind words trying to reassure her.

Galeotti and I, addressing our questions in English to the invisible John King (the table had expressed the wish that we keep speaking English with three raps), stimulated Eusapia to further attempts to operate, and she tried to satisfy our desire, visibly forcing herself to the point of making us feel sorry for her. She usually mumbled: "Help me,"..."I love you"..."Let's go"..."Let's get it"...But these words were rarely followed by proper results, except for table movements mentioned above.

In any case, Galeotti clearly saw something white, diaphanous, like two fingers of an infantile hand approaching his right arm and simultaneously he felt touched. Bottazzi felt a cool breath of air coming from the left while he was near Pansini, who was guarding the *medium*. It seemed to be coming from inside the cabinet, swelling the curtain which flung several times suddenly against the séance table.

Invisible hands touched Pansini more often than anyone else for the whole time he was in contact with the *medium*. I have already mentioned how these touches excited him up to the point of making him cry out. He explained later that the cries were not out of fear, but rather out of being tickled. Be that as it may, these reactions by Pansini stimulated a lot of mediumistic activity in Eusapia. It is impossible to say how, but perhaps one should not neglect that all participants were compelled to unanimously focus their attention only on one thing. In so doing, they reached the homogeneity of intents of the mediumistic chain which seems necessary to the manifestation of relevant phenomena. They were produced precisely in between these touches and the respective motor and vocal reactions by Pansini. The curtain moved as if by currents of air noted by those sitting nearby, and the movements of the table became stronger and more evident, as if moved by invisible hands.

Scarpa, Pansini, and Bottazzi saw faint lights in the cabinet, but in the first evening we could not exclude that they might have had something to do with the light reflected on the surface of the metronome, or on the balance and the frame of the cylinder, all the more so because their appearance and disappearance could also be explained by the opening and closing of the curtains.

The session ended at 24:00 sharp. To tell the truth, we left without feeling very satisfied.

VI. Second Session (April 20, 1907).

At 21:00, barometric pressure = 763.99; temperature = 13.8°C.

Prof. De Amicis was absent; Prof. Lombardi was substituted by engineer Jona.

Having learned by the events of previous session, I replaced the table in the mediumistic cabinet with a heavy wooden board fixed with iron bars and screws on the left and right wall and on the rear door. But since the immobilized board, if beaten, vibrated a lot, I decided to support its right side with a heavy wooden tripod screwed onto the same board. On the board there were from right to left:

a) the cylinder with blackened paper and the letter-weighing balance;

b) the electric metronome fully uncharged but with the rod free to move;

c) the telegraph key;

d) the pear-shaped elastic rubber connected to the mercury manometer;

e) a glass holding a glass tube partly filled with mercury and sealed at both ends;

f) the mandolin in the back left corner.

Under the board on the left, between the tripod and the wall, I placed a small walnut table without the drawer, weight 7.459 kg, width 0.79 m, and height 0.71 m. On this table, placed obliquely from left to right, there were a drum, the trumpet, a small hairbrush, the hen feather, a flask full of water, and an empty heavy glass.

This time, however, we immobilized the board supporting the objects that we wished to be activated, but not the objects themselves, something we later regretted. The small table under it was left free.

When the chain was formed at 21:00, creaks of the séance table started almost immediately, indicating the presence of Mr. John King. Then, the table itself started to levitate, at first weakly then stronger and stronger, initially on the side Palladino had her hands. Then the whole table was lifted. During this session and also in some later sessions we witnessed a strange movement, like a rolling of the séance table which, rather than tapping its feet on the floor, rubbed them quickly from left to right. Minutillo affirmed he had never observed similar phenomenon in the many sessions he had attended. Translated into psychological language, we interpreted these movements as responses given when in a bad mood due to our persistent questions.

For the whole evening Bottazzi guarded the *medium*'s left side. On her right side was at first Jona and later Pansini.

Not caring about the precise sequence of observed events, I prefer to describe them briefly.

The most relevant motor event was the dragging out of the small table placed under the board in the mediumistic cabinet.

The table described *in toto* a curved line about 1.60 m long, turning from the original position into a position oblique from back to front and from right to left. The curve had the convexity versus the séance table. That was the only possible way to turn the table because the *medium* and the rest of us blocked the opposite way to the right. The way it was pulled out is of extreme interest.

The table started moving by steps, every pull perfectly corresponding to pressures and pulls made by Palladino's hands on our hands (mine and Pansini's). At a certain moment, Palladino stretched her legs over my knees and pushed her feet against Jona's knees, who was on my left. I took Paladino's left hand in my left hand, while my right hand touched her legs. Meanwhile Jona's right hand was on my left shoulder to avoid breaking the mediumistic chain. Eusapia's right hand was guarded by Pansini.

While Palladino was in this position, stronger pulls of the small table started to take place, and finally they pulled it out of the cabinet.

Every pull of the small table corresponded in perfect synchrony with a push by Eusapia's leg against Jona's knees and with the contraction of her thigh muscles. In other words, the *medium* truly executed movements identical to those she should have made, had she wanted to pull out the small table from the cabinet with her visible legs. Only, her legs were not

on the small table, but on Jona's knees, and as her legs
were hitting and pushing, the small table was also hit
and pushed, but by invisible limbs. Scarpa attentively
followed the progressive movement of the small table,
which took place some tens of centimeters away from
him who was the closest one to it.

At a given moment the empty glass on the table was
violently thrown at a distance of about two meters on
the floor (but it didn't break). Passing through the air
over the séance table, it grazed Scarpa's left elbow.
This throw perfectly coincided with a powerful kick
Palladino gave to our poor friend Jona, who considered it an homage to science, the very reason we had
gathered here.

The synchrony of mediumistic phenomena with the
muscle contractions of the *medium*'s limbs seems to
me of major importance, worthy of being greatly valued
by whoever wants to try and find an explanation of
mediumistic phenomena. I will have the opportunity
to underline this synchrony more than once in the
following pages.

No other object, despite its being shaken by the
movements on the small table, was turned over.

We observed the usual curtain movements, and felt
the puffs of cool air coming from the cabinet.

The pear-shaped elastic rubber and one of the pressure switches fell on the floor from the board, but they
were not compressed.

There were many touches by invisible hands. Bottazzi noticed them twice, and felt touched by a finger tip once on his right hand and another time on his rib. Pansini was touched several times, and reacted dramatically in the usual way. Finally, Scarpa asked for his right hand, near the curtain on the outside, to be grabbed. After a few seconds everybody saw the curtain swelling, like pushed by a hand with extended fingers from inside the cabinet, and Scarpa felt his hand grabbed by these invisible fingers. Bottazzi distinctly felt the rubbing of the fabric between two hands. Meantime, the *medium*'s hands were well guarded by me and Pansini, and the contact between Scarpa's hand and the invisible hand occurred at about one meter above Palladino's head.

At a certain moment, Palladino asked me to bring my head close to hers. She placed her forehead on mine, and knocked it three times. Three loud synchronous raps were heard on the séance table, which Lombroso and Barzini called "John's cannon shots."

Innumerable faint blows on the table took place later. They were heard by everyone and coincided with Palladino's light pressing the back of my hand with her index finger.

The synchrony of simultaneous blows by invisible hands on the tables outside and inside the cabinet was also very clear.

We twice saw the apparition of something black, resembling a head and sufficiently distinguished by its profile on the wall illuminated by the faint red light of lamp 3. It stuck slowly out from behind the outer end of the left curtain, high up almost on the curtain top. It remained there for two or three seconds, and then retreated rapidly. It seemed like somebody taking a peek at us, who was scared by our exclamations of wonder and withdrew. Everybody saw the apparition. I was quivering throughout my body!

Towards the end of the session the *medium* became delirious and raving, and uttered incomprehensible sentences. When the session unexpectedly ended at 23:00 and the brightest lamp was turned on, she fell into a fit of hysteria.

When this was over, a charged gold leaf electroscope was brought to the table, and Palladino was asked to put hands above it and make movements as if to press the button but without really doing it. She tried it several times, but the gold leaves did not bend down. She was then shown what would happen if she had really pressed the button, and she was allowed to discharge the electroscope. After it was recharged, Palladino was asked again to discharge it at a distance, but still failed.

No recording instrument was activated, and so we did not get traces.

During the session Galeotti and I invited John, in
Italian, French, or English (these are little concessions
which have to be made to Eusapia's deeply rooted
prejudices), to move the rod of the metronome, to
lower the plate of the letter-weighing balance, to press
the pear-shaped rubber. We gradually explained to
her how these instruments were structured and what
movements she was supposed to do with her hands to
move, lower, or press them. All in vain. She kept saying that *she did not find or see* the objects mentioned,
or that *she did not know* how to do it. Then she complained that the objects *were too far out of her reach*.
In fact, the board was fixed at a height of 1.10 m from
the floor which was higher than any ordinary table.
But the negative results of efforts Eusapia made quite
willingly to please us are of great relevance to me now
that I think of them again, although my friends and I
remained quite dissatisfied at the time.

The same orders were in fact obeyed by Eusapia, as
we'll see, in the later sessions: keys were tapped, the
rod of the metronome was set swinging, etc. Having
not achieved these effects in the first sessions dem-
onstrates, as far as I can see, that Eusapia needed to
learn to make unfamiliar movements with her invisible
hands, the same way she would need with her visible
hands. In other words, when compared to the positive
results I shall describe later, the negative results of

initial experiments highlight the psychic or intellectual element operating in mediumistic phenomena, while the muscular contractions and the observed movements of Palladino's limbs synchronous with mediumistic movements highlight the physiological element.

When the session ended, Eusapia eagerly drank a cup of coffee.

Soon thereafter we collected some urine, and analyzed it the next day. It contained two and a half per thousand albumin, but no trace of sugar.

The urine left in a glass deposited an abundant sediment. When examined in the microscope, it appeared to be almost exclusively formed by mucus-pus particles, epithelial cells of the urinary tract, and uric acid crystals. No kidney cylinders were present.

The photograph reproduced here (Fig. 1) shows the way the recording instruments were arranged in the room adjoining the experiment room during the first, second, and third sessions. The two big accumulators which provided the current needed to activate the electric kymograph cannot be seen in the photo because they were on the floor, but one can see the two big cords between the battery and the rheostat.

The door on the back was the one forming the back wall of the mediumistic cabinet. The electric cords and the rubber tube going through the door are clearly seen.

Figure 1. Some of the recording instruments which were placed in the room next to the séance room.

VII. **Third Session (April 24, 1907).**

At 21:00, barometric pressure = 760.74, temperature = 15.6°C.

Present were Professors De Amicis, Scarpa, Pansini, Bottazzi, and Galeotti; and Mrs. Bottazzi.

Prof. De Amicis remained in custody of Eusapia's right hand and foot throughout the entire session, in custody of her left limbs were in sequence Prof. Galeotti, Bottazzi, Mrs. Bottazzi, and lastly Prof. Galeotti again.

The session started at 21:00 sharp, and it ended at 23:00. It was a short session but full of very important phenomena.

In the mediumistic cabinet the board fastened to the walls and to the back door and the tripod were kept in the same position as at previous session. The small walnut table was substituted with a fir footstool.

On the footstool, not immobilized, were:

a) a Marey receiving tambour with a central button glued in the middle of the rubber leaf, which was more resistant than ordinary leaves routinely used in physiological research. I had attached to it with strong glue a wooden disc, which enlarged the surface on which the invisible hand was supposed to press. The tambour was connected by rubber tubing to the mercury manometer that was on the other side of the door.

b) two pressure switches connected to two Desprez signals situated in the adjacent room. Both the Marey tambour and the switches were fastened to the top of the footstool with zinc strips screwed into the wood.

c) an electric bell was also screwed into the footstool.

d) a round enameled iron plate filled with a 2-cm-thick layer of smooth glazier mastic.

e) a majolica plate also containing glazier mastic.

On the floor, to the right of the footstool and between the tripod's three legs, there was a tambourine with two drumsticks above it. On the tripod lower shelf there was the trumpet, and on the middle shelf the brush and an absorbent cotton wad.

On the board:

f) an additional bell;

g) the usual blackened cylinder with the attached pen of the letter-weighing balance;

h) the glass containing the glass tube filled with mercury;

i) the mandolin leaning against the back door;

j) to its right the slightly charged metronome;

k) the telegraph key.

The metronome and the telegraph key were fastened with screws to the board. On the doorframe there was the switch which could be used to activate at the right moment the circuit of the electric kymograph placed in the other room. On the shelves at the left of the mediumistic cabinet there was, on the top shelf, a bunch of flowers in a glass, the gold leaf electroscope on its left, and still farther to the left a graduated test tube filled with hydrogen peroxide and placed upside down in a porcelain capsule filled with water (all these objects were supported by a cast iron piece). Finally, a small plaster dog. On the middle shelf there were two round terracotta plates containing soft smooth clay.

In front of the metronome there was a box of photographic plates tied with a string and containing small letter molds and little pieces of paper. On the lower level of the tripod, next to the trumpet, was the hen feather.

Under the séance table there was a photographic plate (9×12 cm) with a lead cross on top. These were wrapped in black paper, tied with a string, and fastened with two zinc strips to keep them from falling if the table was moved. Palladino did not see them either before or after the session.

Behind the footstool, leaning against the door, there was a barium platinum-cyanide plate.

The inside small table of the previous session was replaced by the footstool for two reasons. First, to be able to screw objects on it, something we could not do on the small walnut table without damaging it, and second, because I was convinced that the *medium* could not resist the temptation of dragging the small table out of the cabinet, just as she had done the night before. On the other hand, the footstool was more difficult to grasp by her invisible hands, and might not be moved. And that is what happened. There were several loud raps on the footstool, and attempts to shift its position. For a long time we heard noises like an arm and a hand or a foot were tenaciously working on the poor footstool to pull it out. But attempts failed, and the footstool was shifted just a few centimeters. To hear this noise and rubbings by the invisible limb while the *medium*'s attention was fully concentrated on the footstool, sounded like a hand was searching for a good spot to hold but not finding it. In any case, these attempts failed, and the footstool was left in peace. Only then the *medium* finally complied with our entreaties not to wear herself out in vain attempts to pull or overturn the footstool, but to work rather on the objects resting on top of it. Obviously, describing these facts in print may give only a faint idea of what happened and of Eusapia's repetitive attempts. There were her sighs when she felt vexed by failure, and the violent blows on the footstool as if it were being punished for its passive resistance and in response to our pleas not to get lost in such minor things while we were expecting something quite different.

The session started with light from lamps 2, 3, and 4. Almost immediately we heard creaks and quivers of wood on the séance table, which responded with three strong blows (meaning yes) to the question: "John, is it you?"

The quick, energetic answer, and the first marked levitation of the table which soon followed the answer, were good signs and filled us with hope of a session

better than the previous ones. This was also because
Palladino was in a good mood and very pleased by Mrs.
Bottazzi's presence, whom she had met the day before.

I shall describe the observed phenomena by
categories.

Levitations of the séance table and blows to it.

There were numerous levitations. Some of them
lasted a few seconds, some longer. One lasted long
enough to enable Galeotti to count to fifty at a rate
approximately equal to that of a metronome beating
every half second. The table rose about 40 cm from
the floor so that each one of us had time and opportunity to ascertain that the table was completely up in
the air, isolated and separated not only from our hands
but also from those of Eusapia.

It is worth mentioning that at a certain moment
during the session, when many events had already
occurred, Palladino said she wanted to get up from
her chair. So she did, while we remained seated. The
table, as if attracted by her body, also rose without
being touched by her hands, first from her side and
then from the other sides. It remained in the air for a
while as we gazed at it in astonishment, and then fell
down with a crash as Palladino returned to her seat.

The levitations always required a certain time to be
completed, and took place with visible oscillations of

the table. After reaching a more or less stable state, the table remained at the attained height for a while, and finally fell down all of a sudden, abruptly, as if an invisible hand had cut the strings keeping it aloft. If that movement could be recorded, or it could ideally be described by a curve, that curve would be quite similar to that of a muscle tetanus which is often initially incomplete, that is with oscillations, and then becomes complete and finally stops abruptly.

That evening the raps were much stronger and more frequent. They were either spontaneous or as replies to questions addressed to the invisible John. They were given both to the séance table and to the board and footstool inside the mediumistic cabinet. These raps had greatly variable intensity, from very faint and audible only if attention was paid to them, to those which sounded like blows given by a powerful fist. They were always sharper than those given by a finger of our hand or a closed fist. Scarpa wished to put his ear on the table, and clearly heard some which were barely audible to us. They were almost always synchronous with little pressures made by one or several Palladino's fingers on the hands of her custodians. Sometimes blows were synchronous with pressures made by her feet. I already mentioned the ones that were heard as she was hitting her forehead on mine. These blows were to be distinguished from those Palladino produced by beating an object on another, for example a drumstick on a drum, on a table, or on a box, etc., and from those produced by making table legs beat rhythmically on the floor, or from other comparable blows.

Apparitions (or materializations).

The presence and activity of mediumistic fingers and hands was revealed not only by blows and movements they produced, but at times also by clear visual sensations. They were pale and diaphanous fingers and hands which might have pearly appearance and brightness. Some appeared above Eusapia's head as if coming from the opening between the two curtains or from their outer edges. In the latter cases they appeared curved, as if they were gathering the edge of the curtain and folding it inwards. But at other times they appeared isolated on the arms or shoulders of people close to the *medium*, while they felt touched, pulled by their clothes, hit, or caressed on their head and face. While in custody of Palladino's left hand, Mrs. Bottazzi saw a black hand and part of a forearm almost touching her right cheek. She was so deeply frightened that she had to abandon her seat and take one farther off, to the visible dislike of Palladino who had many times asked her to stay close to her.

I take this opportunity to mention that the most relevant phenomena in the whole session occurred when Mrs. Bottazzi was in contact with Palladino, as

her mediumistic activity was evidently heightened by
the presence and even more by the closeness of my
wife. Having asked John whether her presence was
welcomed, he answered in a lively way "yes" (three
very strong raps on the table). As a proof of this, the
table was asked to approach her, which it did immediately, oscillating in front of her, like saluting her.
Having asked John if Mrs. Bottazzi was also endowed
with some mediumistic power, he answered quite
energetically twice "yes".

I refer to these details as they clearly demonstrate
the influence people forming the mediumistic chain
have on the *medium*'s activity.

In fact, the most diverse phenomena took place
with extraordinary readiness and swiftness during
the entire session, and all objects and instruments
we had prepared were touched, moved, and put into
action. It also happened that throughout the time Mrs.
Bottazzi was in contact with Palladino, she was not left
in peace a single moment. The curtain swelled around
her several times, like hugging. She was unceasingly
touched, fondled (she said it felt like a cat climbing
up her right arm towards her shoulder), tapped on her
shoulder with something like the open palm of a hand
(and we all heard the blows), and she was the one who
saw the largest number of apparitions.

Hence, it was clearly quite justified that at a certain
moment she felt the need to get away from the sphere

of mediumistic action to avoid these a bit too violent and dramatic demonstrations by the *medium* that corresponded to the sympathy Eusapia had shown to my wife.

While all these events were taking place, Palladino was in a deep *trance*. She mumbled incomprehensible words, was heavily sighing, and did not answer questions. Her face was transfigured, her body muscles were relaxed, and her limbs were immobile under our attentive eyes.

Touches

There were numerous touches, almost always on people in contact with the *medium*, but also on those who approached the *medium* and the curtain with an outstretched arm and asked to be touched or to have their hand grabbed.

More than once the arm of Prof. De Amicis was not only touched, but forcefully pulled as if by an invisible hand coming from the mediumistic cabinet. At a certain moment one of us asked if the spirit of a dead person who was very dear to him could come to us and give him a kiss. The left curtain became restless, swelled out, and swirled around his body as if to hug him, and he felt another face on his face and a mouth kissing him. At the same time Palladino's mouth was posed like kissing, and at one time she smacked a kiss which we all clearly heard. A prejudiced person would suspect a fraud, but would himself become the victim of an error. In the first place the sound of kisses given by invisible lips was also heard when the *medium* only made the act of kissing without any sound. In addition, what I said is to be interpreted only as a phenomenon analogous to that of the synchrony between blows tapped on the table and the light pressures by the *medium*'s fingers on her custodian's hands. Any mediumistic event was almost always occurring simultaneously with movements of one or more parts of the *medium*'s body, whether noticed or not (at times they were very weak or they were made by muscles which were not under the custodian's hand). This means that a kiss given by invisible lips might at times correspond to an analogous movement by the *medium*'s lips, sometimes accompanied by a sound. That no fraud was involved is further demonstrated by the fact that in no way did the *medium* try to emphasize this really impressive event. When all this occurred, Eusapia was in a *trance* and she did not seem to hear our words of amazement over this wonderful event.

When Bottazzi and Galeotti were in custody of the *medium*, they were also touched several times on their arms and breasts. Stretching his right arm and hand towards the curtain, while holding Palladino's left hand with his left hand, Bottazzi clearly felt his hand bumping against a fist.

Pansini's right hand, stretched similarly towards the curtain, was seized and held so tightly that he could not hold back an exclamation of amazement. Scarpa had a similar experience, and also Mrs. Bottazzi while she was far from Palladino. When the curtain was approaching an outstretched hand, anyone looking tangentially at the curtain protrusion distinctly noticed that the curtain was not swelling as when a puff of air was coming from the cabinet. Rather, the curtain showed the irregular profile of stretched fingers of a hand pushing the curtain outwards from inside the cabinet. These fingers eventually grasped the outside hand. When our hand was thus grabbed, simply held for a moment or even pulled towards the cabinet, we felt the contact of a real hand, bony, muscular, most of the times neither hot nor cold, but sometimes warm, in short like a hand of flesh, bones, and blood. To whom did the hand belong which appeared more than half a meter above Palladino's head while her visible hands were rigorously in custody of those closest to her?

Was it the hand of a monstrously long limb budding out of the *medium*'s body, which then vanished, eventually to 'materialize' again?

Was it something similar to an amoeba pseudopodium which comes out of its body, then retreats, and later comes back out again in a different place?

What a mystery!

Objects brought over.

The first object to be brought to the séance table was a small hairbrush. It was placed on the table so quietly that we barely noticed it.

But a bit earlier the trumpet had been thrown to the floor, where it moved, was displaced, and dragged for a while, as if someone was unsuccessfully trying to grab it. But the trumpet was not brought to the table despite our requests.

At one point we heard beats on the little drum which sounded like they were produced by sticks. But we clearly heard the sticks being thrown away while the beating continued. The little drum was then dragged out of the cabinet, upturned, and rolled to the right. We heard a little melody. Lamps 3 and 4 were turned on throughout. The fingers of Palladino's left hand were beating the rhythm on Galeotti's hand in perfect synchrony with the sound of the tambourine. All this lasted quite a while: Palladino was amusing herself and so were we. We asked the tambourine to be brought to the table. Under a bright enough light to distinctly see the tambourine in the right corner near Galeotti, Palladino said to him: "Take it."

Galeotti stuck out his right hand together with the *medium*'s left hand towards the harmless instrument which was meekly resting near his chair, as if attempting to grab it but still remaining at consider-able distance. The tambourine suddenly moved, rolled a little, rose up — as I clearly saw being close to Galeotti — and tried to get up on the table. But it fell, tried again, and fell again, as if it didn't have enough strength to take flight. Worth mentioning was the next event ascertained by Galeotti and myself. When Palladino told him to grab it, the tambourine was fully uncovered by the curtain. But before starting to move and rise up, the free end of the curtain became restless, licked the tambourine, and partly enveloped it as if to help raise it. After the session we also found the hen feather on the table, but nobody had seen it approaching or heard it settling, evidently because of its lightness.

On the far right of the upper shelf there was a bunch of flowers at a distance of more than one meter from the séance table. We had repeatedly asked flowers to be brought to the table, indeed to be offered to Mrs. Bottazzi. At a certain moment the table asked for total darkness, and we turned off light 4. Soon thereafter we heard a strong shaking of the curtain all the way up to the rings by which it was hung on the horizontal rod. An instant later the bunch of flowers grazed Galeotti's face, who at the moment was in custody of Eusapia's left arm, passed by my breast and over my hands which got wet of dripping water, and landed on Mrs. Bottazzi's lap, who was on my left side. Due to darkness, we did not understand at first what had happened, then one after another we exclaimed: "the flowers, the flowers!" The light was turned on. We were not wrong. Galeotti and De Amicis assured that Eusapia's hands had not slipped out of their custody. Bringing out the flowers was a most wonderful event and also an important one, as the bunch of flowers was outside the mediumistic cabinet.

But a moment earlier another equally important phenomenon had occurred, not of lesser importance. We had often requested to move the instruments inside the cabinet: balance, metronome, electric keys, etc. Palladino had not seen these instruments, neither did she know how they looked. I described them, one after another, and minutely explained the way to operate them (having left John aside, I was speaking with Eusapia and teaching her how to operate the instruments). Palladino listened, or at least she seemed to listen to my explanations: for sure, every now and then she replied: "I don't know!...I don't know how to do it!...What should I do to make it move?"

Evidently, she strained herself trying to make new movements with her invisible hands but failing to do so.

Finally, as if putting an end to her useless attempts, the letter-weighing balance came to be obliquely placed on the table while its plate fell on the floor. It had been wrapped by the right curtain, and had skimmed over Mrs. Bottazzi's bosom, who was in contact with Palladino. Seeing it arrive, it looked like it was held by a hand inside the curtain, the curtain being between the invisible hand and the balance.

Another object that was brought out, but in a different manner, was the majolica plate containing mastic. At a certain moment from the outer edge of the left curtain there appeared a round whitish body.

"What is it?" many people exclaimed, but no one understood: some said it was a big fist, some others called it a head. The body retired into the cabinet and disappeared, but after a few seconds it reappeared again, and those closest to it, De Amicis and Scarpa, saw it was a plate. Scarpa got up, stretched out his arm (the plate was high up), grabbed it, and placed it on the table. He told me that when he took it he felt no resistance. The plate seemed floating in the air. Lights were turned on, and we looked to see if marks had been left on it. There were none except those made by Scarpa himself with his finger on the edge of the mastic when grabbing the plate. The plate was put on the séance table. Then the *medium* asked for less light. All lamps were turned off, and at this moment the bunch of flowers was brought over.

When it was dark again, Palladino wished to squeeze my right hand with her left. Under our two hands was Galeotti's left hand. He was her custodian and his right hand was placed on the *medium*'s knees. It should be recalled that Palladino's right hand was being held by Prof. De Amicis. I then felt a soft and cool body on the back of my right hand. I initially thought they were the flowers come back to me, but I eventually realized that it was the plate turned upside down with mastic below and placed horizontally on my fist, which left a mark on it. That mark is the middle one in the following photograph, while marks on the sides are those left by Scarpa's and other persons' fingers. Having placed the plate back on the table, after a few seconds it was brought back on my fist, which had remained in the previous position. But this time the mastic was facing up. When the light was suddenly turned on, everyone saw the plate horizontally balanced on the back of my hand.

This phenomenon closely resembled one of those events that are made by a magician. The conditions under which it took place (complete darkness, three hands entangled together on one side) were such as to raise doubt in the mind of the most fervent believer in mediumistic phenomena. It was Palladino who requested the three hands to be kept together (her left hand, Galeott's left hand, and my right hand) not to interrupt the chain. Surely this was the most favorable situation to substitute her hand with Galeotti's hand on my hand, to free her left hand and grab the plate. But I am definitely sure I never let go off Palladino's hand, and Galeotti confirmed that with his left hand he was simultaneously feeling the presence of two hands in contact with his own.

At the same time, De Amicis was asked if he had always kept contact with Eusapia's right hand, and he answered "Always!"

We asked John to continue moving different objects placed in the cabinet: electric keys, metronome, mandolin, etc. In fact, John was back there! We heard him searching for the objects on the table inside: the glass containing the small glass tube with mercury was shaken and moved, but later abandoned, as John amused himself with the glasses, especially if filled with liquid. The two little bells made some faint jingling. But finally the mysterious hand found the mandolin and started strumming it.

"Bring it here, bring it here," begged De Amicis.

And here was the mandolin, held by its neck by what looked like a hand enveloped by the curtain, which passed between the heads of Palladino and De Amicis and landed on the séance table where under our attentive eyes a marvelous event took place. Eusapia's hands in custody of De Amicis and Galeotti were not on the table, but on her thighs where they made continuous irregular movements as witnessed by those two. The mandolin on the table was continuously shaken, moved, strummed on. It almost fell on the knees of Scarpa and De Amicis, but when we begged it not to be thrown to the floor, it stopped. The light was strong enough for all of us to clearly see that no hand was touching the instrument. So, who was moving it, making its strings to vibrate, and dragging it to the table under our eyes?

Soon afterwards we heard the sound of the metronome. A few beats, then a stop, beats again. The rod was moving and stopping according to our requests. Meanwhile the instrument was strongly shaken. I, being afraid that John meant to carry it outside the cabinet, asked him not to do it, not for the fear of breaking it, but of pulling off the wires relaying Desprez-signals to the recording instruments. Had that happened, we would not have been able to register its movements. The metronome was left in the cabinet, but the shakes it made were strong enough to spill out the mercury from the well (we found mercury sprinkled over the board and the well empty). Thus the beats could not be further recorded. In fact, the trace just above the time trace (Figs. 2 and 3) shows only six beats on the left corresponding to six full oscillations (since only one well contained mercury, contact was established every two beats), then another beat further on and two additional ones close to one another. Finally, to the far right there is at first an irregular trace which could have been made only by pulling the metal cables, and after that three beats of irregular shape. At that point the metronome must have been moved and the mercury spilled out of the well. As a result, successive movements and stops of the metronome rod according to Galeotti's command were no longer recorded. We should have fastened the instrument on the board or we should have used another instrument with different contacts than mercury contacts. But it is always the same story: experience itself teaches how to modify experimental conditions in the most suitable way.

In subsequent sessions this inconvenience was eliminated.

The telegraph key was struck several times. It had been screwed on the wooden board and could not be moved. We all clearly heard the typical sounds of energetic, quick hits. To certify that it was not an illusion,

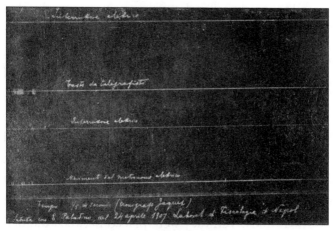

Figure 2. Third session. Traces left by the telegraph key and the electric metronome (labeled as Tasto da telegrafisti and Movimenti del metronome elettrico). Bottom trace, time (marks every 1/5 of a second). No signal was recorded from the electric switch (Interruttore elettrico).

Figure 3. Third session. Continuation of the traces shown in Figure 2.

or a collective hallucination, the second trace from the top (Figs. 4 and 5) shows three groups of signals and two isolated beats in between them. Fortunately, electromagnetic signals function very differently than our senses and cannot deceive or be deceived. The small vertical lines, almost merging with each other as they took place at very short intervals (less than ⅕ of a second) due to the low speed of the cylinder, undoubtedly correspond to the lowering or raising of the key. Looking closely with a magnifying glass (on the originals), one could see that the marks close to each other followed a frequency of about two and a half per one fifth of a second, that is about 13 per second.

The two switches fastened on the footstool were not pressed: the two corresponding traces showed no vertical lines. Yet, they were placed between the bell whose jingle was heard, and the Marey tambour that was activated. Perhaps their surface was too small and that was why they escaped the invisible hand.

I have already described the Marey tambour that
was fastened to the footstool and the way it was connected to the François-Frank mercury manometer.
Every pressure on the wooden disc glued to the elastic
membrane produced a rising of the floating device and
of the manometer pen, while every depression produced a lowering. Now, if you observe the traces (Figs.
4 and 5), you may notice groups of white lines that go
up and down: some higher, some lower. Naturally, the
highest ones correspond to the strongest pressures,
the middle ones to medium intensity, and the lowest
to only faint touches of the disc. Those pressures,
especially the strongest ones, could not have produced

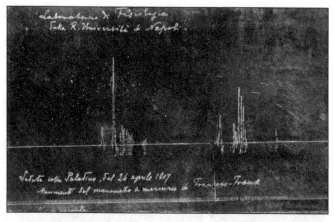

Figure 4. Third session. Top trace, signals recorded from the Marey
tambour. Bottom trace, time (marks every ⅕ of a second). Additional
labelling: top, Physiology lab of the Royal University of Naples; bottom,
Session with Palladino, April 24, 1907. Movements of the François-
Frank mercury manometer.

the highest lines unless exerted on the diaphragm of the tambour that was fastened to the footstool. As to the movements of the footstool and the beats on it, the movements of the rubber tube or some pressures on it, the first ones have no effect, and the last ones produce only small signs, small vertical lines on the manometer's trace. Hence, an invisible hand or foot must have pressed the diaphragm of the receiving tambour, and with great force. The following day I felt convinced that to obtain the highest peaks the disc had to have been pressed to a maximum degree.

This phenomenon, graphically recorded on the rotating blackened cylinder, is of the greatest importance, not only because there can be no doubt about it, but also because it shows that the invisible hand had operated with considerable skill. One is not dealing here with the usual pulling or pushing of a chair or table. To press the disc the mysterious hand had first

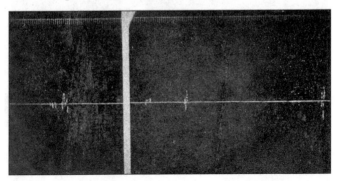

Figure 5. Third session. Top trace, time; middle trace, continuation of the trace shown in Figure 4.

of all to find it, as the surface was relatively small, and then to choose from many possible movements only one, to press the disc down. The mysterious hand might have taken off the disc which was simply glued to the elastic membrane, or perhaps have removed the tambour from the footstool, etc. But that hand simply pressed the disc, obeying my orders to the *medium*, letting it be guided by my description of the little instrument and by instructions I gave to the *medium*, telling her what and how to press to make it function.

Consider this: I spoke to the *medium*, who might never have seen a Marey tambour in her life, and certainly not the modifications I had made. She had not inspected the mediumistic cabinet before the session, and did not know where the instrument was. Her visible hands remained always in contact with her custodians, but they were not resting, rather they kept moving as if searching and touching. On the other side, at a distance of about one meter and on a different level from the *medium*'s visible hands, in the cabinet behind her body another invisible hand with mysterious fingers searched on the footstool, found the object I described, and made the movement suggested by me. Wasn't this a marvelous phenomenon, since it was absolutely excluded that one of Palladino's visible hands had left the custodians' grip, had gone behind her, and had touched and pressed the disc? One should consider that this was not an instantaneous movement. The first group of movements by the manometer's pen at the left comprised three minor groups lasting about thirty-five fifths of a second, that is seven seconds. During all this time her custodian, for example Prof. De Amicis, should have been the victim of an illusionary feeling of contact with the hand in his custody, while in reality the hand was somewhere else. But to admit it, one would also have to assume that Prof. De Amicis had suddenly been hit either by a serious disturbance of his tactile sensibility, or that for seven seconds his attention and surveillance had been completely suspended. Indeed, the possibility of substituting the hand is fully excluded, because at the same time Galeotti had in his right hand the left hand of Prof. De Amicis, and those two left hands cannot possibly be confused even when lights are out.

On the mastic kept in the metal plate we found several impressions of two fingertips made by fingers held together. One peculiar feature worth noticing was that on the mastic, in correspondence to each mark, one could clearly see not lines of skin, but a grid corresponding perfectly to the trace left by the curtain fabric, as we later ascertained. The fingers which left the marks had not touched the mastic directly, but through the curtain fabric. This was confirmed next day when the curtains were examined, and the left curtain was found to have whitish spots of dried mastic.

The enameled metal plate placed on the footstool was quite far from Palladino's body, and the footstool was not moved more than one or two centimeters from where it was at the start of the session, as shown in the photograph of the room that was taken the following morning (Fig. 6). To reach it by her hands, Palladino would have needed either to bend far backwards towards the inside of the cabinet, and we would have noticed it, or she would have had arms which could be elongated or shortened telescopically, as Barzini humorously suggested.

What then?... But let us now continue relating the observed events. We'll draw conclusions at the end.

It is time to describe the experiments we prepared but which did not give positive results.

However much I begged Palladino to touch and rotate the vertical cylinder in the right back corner of the cabinet (Fig. 6), and however much I explained what to do, since she kept saying she didn't understand and could not do it, the

Figure 6. Third session. The mediumistic cabinet as it was found at the end of the session. The dish of mastic on the footstool was in the cabinet, the trumpet was on the floor.

cylinder failed to move except a few centimeters when the letter-weighing balance was detached from it and brought over to the séance table. It was certainly during this movement that the pen, scraping a bit on the blackened paper, left some irregular white marks on it. The paper presenting these spots was fixed, but I don't reproduce the image here, as it has no value.

The photographic plate fastened under the séance table was not impressed despite the fact that Palladino's hands had approached it several times from above during the entire session.

At the end of the session, after the charged gold leaf electroscope was placed in front of Palladino, she was unable to discharge it without touching it.

However, as if to compensate her failure (apparently she did not know that there was no real compensation), a few minutes after the session while she was lying down on the couch in the same room, she asked for the mandolin and laid it down on Mrs. Bottazzi's knees. She placed her fingers to both sides of the neck of the instrument at a distance of 4 or 5 centimeters and made the chords vibrate repeatedly. Only the three of us were present, as the others had hurried to the adjoining room to see if the recording instruments had worked.

But that was not all. Eusapia seemed unsatisfied by what she had accomplished. That evening the session did not appear to have been sufficient to let her discharge all that which in mediumistic jargon is called *fluid*, an expression in any case reminding of times not so far back when heat, electricity, and magnetism were also called fluids. So, Eusapia got up, approached the shelves nervously, and out of the two rods, one of glass the other of ebonite, which served to charge the electroscope, she chose the latter (who knows why *mediums* prefer everything which is black and gloomy!). After placing it in front of her, she held her hands vertically, parallel on both sides of the rod, and by rhythmic movements of lifting and lowering her hands, made the rod follow every movement of her hands as if they were a powerful magnet and the wooden rod was of iron. This experiment, which bears resemblance to what magicians use to do, was made in full light after the session in presence of only two persons, without Eusapia trying to impress her observers since she knew that the most skeptical ones were elsewhere.

Her hands were at a distance of at least 10 centimeters from the rod and yet made it move. Not unlike her fingers which made the strings vibrate at a distance, producing the creaking sound made by nails scraping on mandolin strings.

Some of the phenomena that took place during the third session convinced me that the so-called invisible hands of Palladino resemble her visible hands, not just for the movements they are capable of making, but also for the sensitivity they seem to have.

At a certain moment, while I was in custody of Palladino's left hand, she took my right hand and brought it close to the curtain, asking *what was that hard stone she felt inside*, that is in the cabinet. I did not understand, as there were no stones there.

"Let's go and touch it" I said, and I extended as far as I could towards the board my right arm which was followed by Eusapia's left arm. But I could not even reach the front edge of the board since we were too far away. Later on, when I thought of it again, I assumed that what she felt as a hard stone was the small metal dome of the spring bell which, as shown in the photograph, was considerably more in front of the balance, yet nonetheless was seized and brought to the séance table. I insist on this detail since if I could not reach the bell despite the fact that my arm is a few centimeters longer than Palladino's, how could have she succeeded in grasping the balance that was on the same board at least 20 centimeters behind the bell?

VIII. **Fourth Session (April 27, 1907).**

At 21:00, barometric pressure = 751.69, T = 17.3°C.

Present were Professors De Amicis, Scarpa, Galeotti, Pansini, Bottazzi, and Cardarelli; engineer Jona; and Mrs. Bottazzi.

Awful weather, suffocating sirocco wind blowing. It was cloudy, and the air was almost saturated with humidity. Palladino was in a bad mood, she quarreled at home with some women who pretended to keep her company but were taking advantage of the situation (she was alone with no close relatives except some distant ones on her dead husband's side, of whom she harbored bad memories, not hiding them). She felt utterly irritated. I barely succeeded in convincing her to leave the house, but the presence of my wife calmed her down a bit. In the laboratory where everybody was already waiting for her, she welcomed Senator Cardarelli with sufficient kindness despite the fact that he was new to her sessions. The agreeable countenance and the flattering behavior of that venerable man, who did not consider it inappropriate or diminishing to his reputation to attend these sessions for his love of truth, surely contributed to calming down Eusapia's misoneistic attitude. And a lot also came from her high self-respect. Despite having seen princes and princesses, grand dukes of imperial houses competing to honor her, Eusapia, thanks to her discernment and quick intuition, cared much more for the critical judgment of scientists than for the banal admiration of 'high society,' regardless of what people said to the contrary.

The session started at 21:30, and ended at midnight.

For three quarters of an hour there were no notable events. Eusapia made visible efforts to produce them, also to pay homage to Prof. Cardarelli, but without success. This almost always happens. When a new person attends the session she remains inhibited for a while.

Custodians of Eusapia's hands and feet were Senator Cardarelli on one side for the entire session, and at first Mrs. Bottazzi on the other side. She, however, had to leave her post because, like the previous night, she soon became the main target of John King's rude caresses: she was enveloped by the curtain, was touched, slapped on her back, etc. Later on, Prof. Bottazzi and ultimately Prof. De Amicis were Palladino's guardians.

The mediumistic chain was not always strictly maintained. In addition to two breaks requested by Palladino, Bottazzi, Galeotti, and Scarpa moved around frequently and went out of the room, either to activate cylinders in the adjacent room or to look for a little rope requested by Eusapia, or for different reasons. Our sessions were always characterized by a certain restlessness in some of us, which shocked an orthodox spiritualist (see the report of the seventh session). But this was quite natural. The spiritualist attended sessions being already willing to admire. Full of faith (bless him!) like every believer, nothing stirred his mind, while in our minds there were doubts. They have not left me even today as I am writing these lines, and have been present in many sessions where I have seen phenomena take place with no possibility of fraud. The doubt made many of us leave the mediumistic chain to become external observers, as if wanting to escape the sphere of the *medium*'s action where it could not be absolutely excluded that a hypnotic and suggestive influence was being practiced. During the first session, Scarpa was Eusapia's pet hate, and she was irritated rather than bewildered under his surveillance. On the other hand, I, having already found a place in her heart, approached her right away in a gentle or resolute manner:

"But dear Eusapia, we are here not only to admire the wonderful phenomena you can produce, but also and above all to verify, ascertain, and criticize. Not that we have any doubts about you, we do not suspect fraud, but we want to see, to follow how the phenomena take place. This is why Scarpa is spying on the mediumistic cabinet through the small opening of the curtains, lighting it up with the flash of a harmless pocket lamp."

"Look," I added. "He remains standing on one side or another or in front of the curtains to see better, to command a look like a captain at sea or in a battlefield. What do you prefer, the passive admiration you have already received aplenty, or an objective affirmation by a physicist accustomed to challenging nature to extort the truth still hiding from our eyes?"

In this manner irritable Eusapia softened up, got hold of herself, and did not rebel. She meekly put up with the sharp eyes of that careful observer, who gave up in the end as he never detected a trace of fraud.

Regardless of his post, Scarpa had always the noble task of holding with his hands one or both of Eusapia's feet when she was ready to produce some of the more relevant phenomena or when she had to exert greater strength. In so doing, she certainly believed she was providing him tangible proof of the means she used in mediumistic operations.

While in *trance*, Palladino was quite often not satisfied with her contact with the two custodians, but faintly asked for the hand of a person nearby or wanted him to put his hand on her knees, or asked to place her forehead on the head of one of her custodians. In the end, after her spiritual reconcilement with Scarpa, she not only tolerated his surveillance but often wanted a close personal contact with him. And Scarpa took the opportunity to put his arm around her back pretending to support her while she was tired. Meanwhile he used this privileged position to frequently throw a glance inside the cabinet, and to make sure that Eusapia's tangible and visible arms never penetrated there. During one of these amorous behaviors he saw something behind Eusapia's back which stunned him. But I'll recount this in the report of the sixth session.

Let's go back to the fourth session. I mentioned that it was a bit disorderly. This was mainly due to Palladino's bad mood. She not only felt the need to interrupt the session and have a rest, but also got up three or four times. Twice she asked all of us to stand up and move around the room. While we complied, she succeeded in producing two marvelous levitations of the séance table, which was lifted at about 60 cm from the floor and remained up in the air without Eusapia's hands touching it.

Considerable changes had been made in the mediumistic cabinet. Two electric keys were fastened on the board, one of which was left uncovered while the other one was placed inside a cardboard box turned upside down and fastened to the wooden board by two strips of zinc foil. The covered key was a telegraph key, while the other key was a spring key whose photo is

Figure 7. Fourth session. The electric spring key as it appeared before the start of the session.

shown (Fig. 7), for a reason I will explain later. The electric metronome with mercury was replaced by a metronome with simple metal contacts, the Verdin model, which also has a bell inside, ringing every two simple oscillations of the rod. The test tube filled with hydrogen peroxide was overturned in a glass half full with normal water. In addition, there was a gold leaf electroscope, and next to it the ebonite stick. After having taken the photo of the cabinet, we placed on the left of the board two half-filled glasses, one with a barium chloride solution, the other one with a sodium sulfate solution (if the two liquids are mixed, a white precipitate of barium sulfate is formed). On the right were two small half-filled Erlenmeyer flasks, one with a ferric chloride solution, the other one with a potassium ferrocyanide solution (if the two liquids are mixed, one yellow-reddish the other yellowish, a precipitate of Prussian blue is formed). The barium platinum-cyanide plate was suspended in the middle of the mediumistic cabinet, high up and inclined a little forward.

On the footstool on the left under the board we placed the tambourine, Galeotti's typewriter (in the back), and a new Marey tambour receiver. A metal cannula connected by rubber tube to the Marey tambour was welded laterally to the tambourine, which became a kind of receiving tambour allowing the graphic recording of a small melody just in case John felt like playing one. Moreover, since the membrane of the receiving tambour connected to the mercury manometer of the previous night was too weak and soft, I replaced it with bellows built according to the same principle, but with a more resistant membrane, similar to those used for spreading insecticide powder.

To the right of the footstool there was a chair weighing about 4 kg on which we placed an enameled iron plate with smooth mastic. The chair had been requested by Palladino the previous evening when we asked her to make an imprint on the mastic.

Three separate blackened cylinders were placed in the room with the recording instruments. On the left cylinder, operated by a clockwork mechanism, there were two pens, one connected to the mercury manometer and the other to the Marey receiving tambour. On the middle cylinder, which rotated very slowly, there were the pens of two Desprez signals connected to the electric keys. Finally, on the right cylinder there were two other pens of Desprez signals, one connected to the metronome and the other connected by a long cable to an electric switch resting in Prof. Galeotti's pocket.

The arrangement of six pens writing on three separate cylinders was meant to record their movements on surfaces rotating at different speeds. But the left cylinder could not be activated at the start of the session because its charge lasted only a few minutes. It

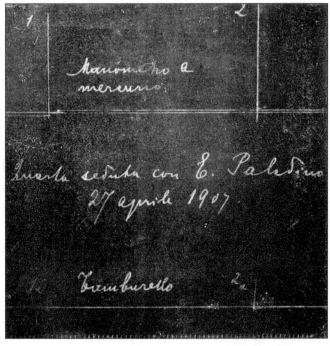

Figure 8. Fourth session. Top trace, signals recorded from the electric metronome; bottom trace, signals recorded from the small drum. Signals 1 and 1a (the latter one quite faint) are the original signals left on the motionless cylinder. Signals 2 and 2a were made by Bottazzi to determine the force needed to produce the recorded signals. The time trace is barely visible at the bottom of the figure. Additional labeling: top, mercury manometer; middle, Fourth session with E. Palladino April 27, 1907; bottom, Small drum.

was then necessary for the laboratory technician to remain in the instrument room and to instruct him to switch it on at our request. But it happened that when the two receiving instruments were put into action, our command was either not heard or not understood.

The cylinder remained motionless and the pens wrote only two vertical lines (Fig. 8) instead of registering all the presses made on the bellows and the melody of the tambourine. Thus, we got proof that everything had to be within the reach of our hands, and that the presence of an extraneous person, although trained for similar tasks, was not of help, but rather complicated things and made results less trustworthy.

Movements and levitations of the séance table, at first irregular and weak, became very relevant. We obtained a levitation lasting about 10 seconds at a height of 30–40 cm and a shorter but higher one while Palladino was the only one standing up. Finally, at the end of the session, an additional levitation occurred that lasted several seconds while all of us were standing up at Palladino's request. On this occasion, the table rose up about one meter and hovered in the air while no one touched it. It is important to notice how much effort one needs during levitations to lower the table by just a few centimeters. Sometimes we tried all together to lower it by pressing its surface with our hands, but without success. It yielded and lowered a little but as soon as we let go our hands it rose up again.

During this session we saw the tiny lights observed earlier by others. According to my visual sensation, similar to that of my colleagues, they looked like little flames resembling those of a candle in size, but shorter and not yellow but purple, brighter in the middle and vanishing at their edges. They looked as though they were coming out of the *medium*'s head and slowly waving up and disappearing in air. They were quite distinct against the black curtain, and did not come back during the rest of the session. During their appearance Palladino remained motionless. Their appearance was not in connection with anything else, nor were they announced in any manner by the *medium*.

Apparitions or materializations were numerous and different. Generally they were never seen by all members of the chain, since to see them clearly depended on their location, their being more or less illuminated by the lamps, and the respective sites of observers. I saw hands and closed fists appearing above Palladino's head between the two curtains. They were sometimes of normal size, but at some other times they were at least three times larger than Palladino's hand and fist. Twice I quickly extended my hand to grasp them because the sitters farther away affirmed that objects were brought over by the same invisible hand, but I was always too late, the apparitions dissolved and I found the place empty.

Another time I saw a black forearm and a white left hand in a horizontal position between Palladino and Prof. Cardarelli, and directed from Palladino to Cardarelli. They seemed to have the dimensions of Palladino's forearm and left hand which, however, Prof. Cardarelli assured us were guarded by his right hand. Twice I saw a black shape appear from behind the free border of the right curtain on Prof. Cardarelli's side halfway up the curtain, hence at a level much higher than Palladino's head. It could have been an enormous fist or a head. Galeotti saw two white, diaphanous fingers settle on his right arm and then disappear. According to him they resembled fingers of an infantile hand.

These apparitions were really strange: fingers, hands, fists, arms, and heads, sometimes white or rather of the color of our skin, a bit diaphanous, translucent, or black like the curtain! They were strange because they seldom appeared to do or to hint at something. Usually they appeared, one might say, only for the sake of being seen. They remained *immobile* for a few seconds, touching or not touching participants, and then they disappeared.

The idea that these bodily human appendages sometimes made their appearance only for the purpose of exhibiting themselves came spontaneously to mind. But at other times they performed physical tasks, moved objects, shifted curtains, etc. They were not always visible to the participants, and for obvious reasons, such as when they remained in the mediumistic cabinet behind the curtains, when they appeared under a chair, stool, or table, or when their apparition was unexpected and fleeting, for instance when they touched you very briefly. In all these instances it is easily understood that they also could not always be seen by us in view of the dim light in the room and the play of shadows of our heads on the walls and on the surface of the séance table. Certainly they preferred to remain hidden. And when they moved forward to touch, carry, or offer an object, or to take back one previously offered, in most cases they remained covered by the curtains. Our eyes nonetheless recognized the relief of an open hand, extended fingers, or closed fists. Nevertheless, the movements (lifting the table, vibrating the mandolin cords, raising or lowering the ebonite stick, etc.) often took place in full light without anybody being able to see an operating hand or finger. As a result, movements seemed to occur in an entirely incomprehensible way.

In these exact cases, lacking the visible or tactile sensation which revealed the moving agent, one renounced the mechanical interpretation of the observed movements, and looked for other explanations like magnetic attractions and repulsions and the like. But in the majority of cases movements occurred as if, since the *medium*'s natural limbs were imprisoned, new additional limbs were generated out of her body, in no way differing from natural limbs.

It is peculiar that materializations of appendages usually lasted for a short while, a few seconds at most. Since the duration of each motor event is also often fairly short, it naturally crossed our minds that the putative mediumistic supernumerary appendages were responsible for the actions perceived by our senses, and that there was an interdependent relationship between these actions and materializations, whether or not they were visible and tangible.

But let's leave the difficult field of hypotheses, interpretations, or representations, and return to narrate events of the fourth session.

Various touches were felt repeatedly by Cardarelli especially, but also by Bottazzi, De Amicis, and Galeotti, that is, as usual, by those in contact with the *medium*. I felt rough fingers and nails on my hands and a finger poking on my face between the root of my nose and the inner corner of my left eye and it hurt a little. Throughout the entire session Cardarelli was the victim of such touches. At first there were small pushes under his chair and on his legs, then strong pulls of his right arm towards the cabinet, at times so powerful that he had to turn his chest to that direction. In addition, he got slaps on his back by an open hand, which everybody heard, and also kisses and pulls of his ear. I saw the right curtain swell out in the shape of a cone, the peak of the cone approaching Cardarelli's cheek or ear. He said to have felt the sensation of a mouth kissing him, or two warm fingers pulling his ear.

An episode with a stethoscope and spectacles was amusing. Prof. Cardarelli had in the right pocket of his jacket a disassembled ebonite stethoscope. When the lights were turned off, I felt first on my face, then on my hands, an object resembling the opening of the trumpet. I said "the trumpet has come to me." But soon that object moved out and later it returned on my fingers. Finally, by touching it, I recognized that it was a piece of the stethoscope. At that, Cardarelli let go of Palladino's hand for an instant, put his hand in his pocket and, not finding the stethoscope, exclaimed: "It is my stethoscope, somebody removed it while I did not feel any touches, despite my being very alert. Give it back to me!" And soon the stethoscope moved against his lips and — everyone hearing it! — knocked on his teeth. Cardarelli clasped it with his teeth, but realized that a piece was missing. He grabbed it with his left hand while keeping it tight with the additional help of Jona's right hand, and asked the missing part to be returned to him. It was then brought back to him, but at the same time a mysterious hand forcefully ripped away the whole stethoscope from Cardarelli's and Jona's hands. During this last act the stem of the instrument was slightly bent.

"Among the several touches and kisses" (this is how Prof. Cardarelli described the episode of the spectacles to me) "which I announced every time although everybody heard them, on one occasion when

my forehead was strongly rubbed, the *pince-nez* I wear
without a string fell on my knee. I thought it had fallen
on the floor and soon I told it to John. A little later I
distinctly felt the most delicate touch on my thighs,
like a hand searching for something. And at once
my spectacles were placed on my nose with an exact
movement. Useless to say, during all this I kept tight
control of Palladino's hand."

One should consider that to assemble and disassem-
ble a stethoscope and to replace a pair of spectacles on
the nose are two operations which are hard to perform
with just one hand. A doctor, who does it many times
a day, performs it always with two hands. How could
Palladino do it with only one hand?

Palladino asked her feet to be held and invited
Scarpa to do it, while Cardarelli and Bottazzi guarded
her hands. She started to bend her legs, which Scarpa
attentively followed. At the same time, the chair with
the plate of mastic on top started moving from the
back of the mediumistic cabinet step by step. We all
heard its displacements, which Scarpa assured us were
occurring in synchrony with the movements of her legs.
The chair moved forward, and at a certain moment
the plate fell on the floor. But it did not slide, rather
it overturned when falling, as we later found on the
mastic a deep impression of one of the anterior corners
of the chair and traces of mastic on the corner of the
chair. The chair reached the curtain and through a

major effort of the *medium*'s feet and arms was lifted and brought onto the séance table. Somebody hurried to grab it, but Palladino gave a cry of pain and exclaimed:

"Let go of my chair!"

We complied. The chair started moving on the table, upturned with its back towards the end of the table opposite of Palladino, and fell down from that side almost into Mrs. Bottazzi's lap. If one keeps in mind the initial situation of the chair, and the way it was brought to the table, one is compelled to admit that Palladino could not have used feet or hands to perform the difficult movements required, unless by prejudice he is willing to deny the reality of facts. None of us, even those situated at an arm's length of the chair, would have been able to touch it with his hands, to grab it behind his shoulders, to lift it and bring it to the table. As I said, the plate did not slide from the chair, but it upturned and was thrown to the floor, as if to make the chair lighter. The next day I reproduced this phenomenon, and ascertained that the plate had to slide whichever way the chair was moved, and had to be overturned to present the mark of the corner of the chair on the mastic.

As previously mentioned, two Erlenmeyer flasks were in the mediumistic cabinet. At a certain moment, the curtain started to stir and the flask containing the iron chloride solution was dragged out, landing on the séance table with the curtain, while not a drop spilled out.

We had asked Eusapia several times to play the tambourine. At last, we heard it moving and falling to the floor. Soon thereafter we heard it being played. Those in charge of Palladino's hands verified that the strokes on the tambourine were synchronized with faint movements of her hands. We were hoping to find a trace of the melody on the cylinder but, as mentioned, the cylinder was still and we found only a single vertical line (Fig. 8).

Even assuming that Cardarelli and Bottazzi were victims of hallucination, that they believed to feel little taps on their hands by Eusapia's fingers while her fingers were actually in contact with the tambourine, it would have been necessary for Palladino's body to be considerably inclined backwards and towards the floor to reach the tambourine. Indeed, as mentioned, the small drum had been thrown down from the stool, and most likely could not have been within her reach. How would all the other participants not have noticed the abnormal position of Palladino's body? Were they all

Figure 9. Fourth session. The electric spring key as it appeared at the end of the session (to be compared to the photo shown in Figure 7).

hallucinating? But then, hallucination becomes a very convenient way of explaining everything.

Bellows were also pressed, but the manometer pen wrote only one vertical line since the cylinder failed to rotate (Fig. 8).

I later reproduced the movements of the two pens artificially to check how much pressure had to be exerted on the tambourine and on the membrane of the bellows: these two traces are reproduced on the same Figure 8, on the right.

Keys of the typewriter were pressed more than once but no letters were printed on the sheet, evidently because the pressure on the keys was not strong enough, as also judged by what we heard. Twice we heard the sound of fingers moving along the keyboard, as if typing rapidly. Note that the typewriter was placed on a stool in the back of the cabinet.

The electric spring key shown in Figure 7 not only was pressed many times, but it was deformed, as can be seen in Figure 9, showing the way the key was found after the session. To deform it in such a manner, one first needs to twist the key and then to press its upper button forcefully down. In so doing, having lost the contact point below, the button is pressed down to an empty space and the spring is bent, as seen in the Figure. It is impossible to displace the spring laterally without holding the base of the key steady with another hand. The spring was firmly fastened to one of the two small wire-holding columns by the overlying piece screwed on the column axis. But one has to admit as well that once the spring was twisted laterally, even by a little bit, the mere hitting of the key might produce only further displacement. According to this second hypothesis, which I prefer to hold, the involvement of two hands becomes unnecessary. Certainly, the deformation of the key had to happen during the first hits, since the large number of hits we heard does not correspond to the few traces made by the electromagnetic device on the cylinder (Fig. 10, top trace). The reason is clear: when the upper button does not hit the button below it, no electric contact is made, no matter how many beats are made.

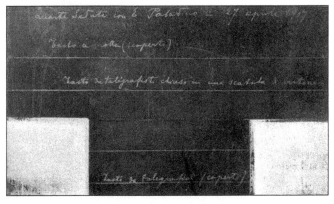

Figure 10. Fourth session. Top trace, signals obtained from the spring key; middle trace, lack of signals from the telegraph key enclosed in the cardboard box; bottom trace, continuation of the top trace. Additional labeling: top, fourth session with E. Palladino — April 27, 1907; top trace, spring key (not enclosed); middle trace, telegraph key enclosed in a cardboard box; bottom trace, telegraph key (enclosed).

As an additional consequence of the deformation of the key, some marks on the cylinder corresponded to persistent contacts rather than to single hits. Most likely on those occasions the upper button was made to touch and be removed from the lower button by lateral movements. I artificially reproduced these marks by inducing lateral movements of the deformed key.

After several requests the metronome was set going (Fig. 11), but stopped after a few swings since its charge was low. While it was going, Palladino was asked to stop it, but she failed. Actually, as we later found, it was not easy to stop it since a new fairly strong spring had been put into its clockwork mechanism. In some points of the trace reproduced here some irregularities are present which might be also attributed to attempts to stop the rod of the metronome.

Figure 11. Fourth session. Top trace, signals obtained from the electric metronome. Irregularities shown at the arrow indicate interferences with rod oscillations; bottom trace, time. Additional labeling: top, fourth session with E. Palladino — April 27, 1907.

As mentioned above, Galeotti was holding in his hand a small electric switch that was connected by a

long cord to the Desprez signal coming from the metronome. Galeotti meant to operate the switch at each
command given by the *medium* to stop the metronome
and restart it. This would have allowed checking which
results corresponded to commands. It is useless to say
that there was no correspondence, as was also shown
by the tracing, which is not reproduced here since the
metronome never did stop. The cord of the switch passing high on the wall was used by the *medium* — that
is by John — only to have a bit of fun. Indeed, at a
certain moment during the session he started pulling
it as if to seize it. Galeotti kept holding it back while
the other one pulled, until he finally decided to leave
the cord in peace.

IX. **Fifth Session (May 3, 1907).**

At 21:00, barometric pressure (Capodimonte Observatory) = 755.3; temperature = 12.2°C. Relative air humidity = 86%.

Present were Professors Galeotti, De Amicis, Pansini, Cardarelli, Scarpa, and Bottazzi, and engineer Jona.

Lamp 1 was placed high up in the left back corner of the mediumistic cabinet. The pressure switch at the end of a long cord was kept in the pocket of a participant. The lamp was put there without Palladino knowing about it, to illuminate at any moment the inside of the cabinet in order to discover possible fraud. Lamp 4, at first mobile, was fastened to the wall and a rheostat inserted in its circuit to dim the light without turning it off.

The board was taken out of the mediumistic cabinet and substituted by a tripod of massive wood with three shelves immobilized by iron bars. To increase the surface of the top shelf, a rough small wooden board was nailed to it. On the board there was an electric key (T1) inside a little rectangular wooden box stabilized by three screws, two in front and one behind; a second electric key (T2) inside a small perforated zinc box likewise secured to its support by screws; and a third electric key (T3) placed behind the second key, uncovered but screwed into the wood (this was the spring key which the night before was deformed and eventually repaired). To the right of the keys there were two half-filled glasses, each with the capacity of about 100 cm^3, one with a copper sulfate solution, the other one with a potassium ferrocyanide solution (when these liquids are mixed, a reddish precipitate of copper ferricyanide is formed). Behind the glasses was the bellows replacing the Marey receiving tambour that was connected to the mercury manometer. Still farther back was the metronome, and among these objects one stick of the tambourine.

On the middle shelf of the tripod we placed the trumpet and the brush.

On its lower shelf we had two half-filled Erlenmeyer flasks, one with a potassium ferrocyanide solution, the other one with a ferric chloride solution (when these liquids are mixed a precipitate of Prussian blue is formed).

To the right of the tripod a chair was immobilized on the back door. Over it there was a big terracotta plate filled with statuary soft clay.

On the floor we placed the tambourine, a bell, a telegraph key, the ebonite stick, and the mandolin.

In the recording instrument room, we reset everything the way it was in the first sessions; that is, we had the two cylinders of the Straub electric kymograph, one on top of the other. On the upper cylinder we put the two pens, connected to the Marey tambour and the mercury manometer, respectively. On the lower cylinder we placed the four Desprez signals connected to the three keys and to the metronome. The kymograph could be activated by me whenever needed.

Two photographic plates wrapped in black paper and tied with a string were placed on the middle shelf of the experiment room, near the flower vase.

Galeotti, Scarpa, and I decided that this session had to be devoted to the detection of fraud, if any, and to the elimination of any doubt from our minds. Accordingly, we placed all objects in the cabinet within Palladino's reach, as if to lure her, and the lamp to illuminate the inside at the right moment.

Galeotti and I were in custody of the *medium*'s limbs for almost the entire session, determined not to be replaced by anybody else. Scarpa assumed for himself the task of leaving the chain every now and then to place himself in the best possible position to keep his surveillance. I placed myself on the left side of Palladino (she is left handed and prefers to *work* with her left limbs), and did not leave my post. Galeotti was on her right, and only at the end of the session, when we became convinced of the reality of phenomena, did he ask Prof. Cardarelli to replace him.

Towards the middle of the session, Palladino, as if sensing our suspicions, invited Scarpa to her side. He placed himself between the *medium* and me, and wrapped his arm around her back, thus doubling the surveillance on her left side where there was more fear of her freeing her arm.

The session started at 21:00 sharp. Eusapia was in a good mood.

De Amicis was a bit late. He arrived a few minutes after John revealed his presence. We asked the séance table to salute the newcomer. The table started moving soon thereafter, levitated, rapped the floor, and approached him, throwing itself not very politely at him.

I did not mention the levitations of the table which took place either with or without imposition of the *medium*'s hands, the raps on the floor and on the table by invisible hands, the movements and swellings of the curtains, and the first touches on my arm and chest. I just want to point out that the first movements of the curtain took place mainly on the right, that is on the side corresponding to Palladino's left side.

At first the mandolin was only touched, later strummed upon. Eusapia, complying with the wish of De Amicis, wanted to take it and bring it to the table. She started to make small movements with her shoulder, arm, and left hand. I noticed and followed them carefully. They resembled those she would have made with the natural limb, had it been free and had she been able to use it to grab the instrument placed on her left side. Meanwhile Scarpa approached me, stood right behind my chair, and distinctly saw the mandolin move, rise, fall down, and overturn, *without a hand touching it*, in a light more than sufficient to detect every movement by Palladino's arms. Palladino, extending her left hand and my associated right hand towards the floor where the mandolin was, said to me: "Let's take it... help me... " and made an effort as if to grab and lift it, as if to grab something with fingers. Meanwhile the mandolin, wrapped in the curtain, rose up a little from the floor, but fell down again with its convexity up, and Eusapia exclaimed in her dialect with visible anguish: "it slipped!... ". But the failure only stimulated her. She tried again, but without success. Since I felt sorry for her, I tried to divert her from these useless attempts to bring the instrument to the table, but she seemed obsessed with this idea and continued without paying attention to me.

It would be necessary to have had Palladino's fingers in your own hand, like I had that evening, to be convinced that the movements of the mandolin (rising, dragging on the floor, overturning, strumming, etc.) were all synchronized with the most delicate movements of her fingers, with pulls and pushes of the *medium*'s hand, as if her hand had been directed in the execution of the movements by a will that knew the effect to be produced. They were not irregular, impulsive, disorderly movements. They were precise and coordinated movements done by one or more fingers, identical to those one would make if trying to seize or to strum the strings with precision and delicacy. Scarpa and I had our eyes fixed on the mandolin and we can affirm with certainty that the instrument, well lit by the lamp above, was not touched by Eusapia's visible hands, and that they were indeed at least 50 centimeters away. The mandolin moved by itself, as if it had magically been provided with motor organs. It looked like a carcass of a monstrous reptile restored back to life. There is no way of describing the sensation one experiences when seeing an inanimate object move, *and not just for a moment but for several minutes in succession,* moving without anybody touching it, while everything around was still, under the influence of a mysterious force. Finally, the mandolin was left in peace, but Palladino was only partly satisfied. On the other hand, I was quite satisfied, since simply bringing the mandolin onto the table would have deprived us of the long and detailed examination we were able to make of the correspondence between the *medium*'s intentional movements and the movements of the object on which invisible limbs were acting.

We heard an object fall on the floor; it could have been paper. It was the package of the photographic plates we had placed on the shelf. When developed next day, we found they had not been minimally impressed.

Eusapia opened my right hand, stretched my three middle fingers, and pressing and rubbing my fingertips on the table, she said to me in a faint voice: "It is so hard!...what is it?" I did not understand, and she added: "There, on the chair...what is it?"

Figure 12. Fifth session. Imprint of three fingers on statuary soft clay.

And I rushed to say: "It's the clay; make an impression of a face." "No," she answered." "It is hard, too hard; take it away." "The chair as well?" "No, leave the chair." To satisfy Eusapia's wish, somebody left the mediumistic chain for a moment, took a look at the dish, and saw a mark of three fingers. With a more accurate examination made the next day, we noticed that the impressions (Fig. 12) seemed to have been made by the rubbing of three fingers. They evidently corresponded to the comparable movement made by Eusapia's left hand when she pressed my fingers on the table. In the margin of the middle impression one clearly saw the mark of an electric cord. It is hard to explain how that occurred. The cord of the lamp placed in the mediumistic cabinet was surely hung over the back of the chair holding the soft clay plate.

Perhaps, the cord contacted the clay when the plate was taken away. In this, as in several other occasions, it is worth noting the coincidence between the *movement* made by Palladino's left hand and the sensation she mentioned of feeling something hard. *So, the medium not only moves but also feels with her invisible appendages, as I previously said.* While the movement took place on her left, the phenomenon occurred on the right of Palladino's body. The crisscrossing of the *medium*'s movements and the observed effects by mediumistic operations, already noted by others, was also observed by us several times.

Now Eusapia started to *work* on the chair freed from the weight of the plate. Propping up her left foot against my right foot and her right foot against Galeotti's left, she made efforts to push. The chair moved, approached the séance table, and rose up. It looked like it was trying to climb up on the table with its back inclined forward partly wrapped in the curtain. After repeated efforts, it succeeded. We exclaimed in chorus: "Bravo! Bravo!" We asked her: "Should it be taken away?" "No! no!" Eusapia answered, "Leave the chair to me." While the chair was standing on the table, other phenomena took place, which I will describe.

At a certain moment the chair started moving again. It fell upside down over the corner of the table between

Palladino and me, to the floor in the direction of the mandolin. Later, Scarpa used the chair for sitting without Palladino's objections. It seemed that she had forgotten. It is peculiar, however, that soon after an object is brought to the séance table, Eusapia gets irritated and shows vivid annoyance if somebody tries to touch or take it away, as if the object became part of her, or a very sensitive part of her remained tightly connected to the object for a while.

Eusapia's mediumistic limbs penetrated into the cabinet, after having practiced on objects outside, and started an activity we could hear but not see. I begged my friends not to distract the *medium* with requests of touches, apparitions, etc., and converge their desires and wills only on the things I asked to be executed. The *medium* threw away the trumpet, the brush, and the ebonite stick. They fell on the floor, and after being moved and dragged a few times were left in peace.

The cord of the lamp inside the cabinet, which, as the chair was lifted to the table, fell to the floor and was placed on the back of Galeotti's chair, was pulled out from the cabinet, and then violently thrown with the switch on the séance table. I hastened to request participants not to touch it, but did not explain that pressing it would turn on the lamp in the cabinet, a thing known only by Galeotti, Scarpa, and me. But what we did not do, was done by the *medium*. The switch was carried away and thrown to the floor. Eusapia was in an extraordinary state of tension. Her eyes were wandering, and she was making small movements with her fingers. She seemed to be looking for something, but nobody knew where. Her attitude was that of a blindfolded person searching the space around him with his hands in hope of finding a lost object. At a given moment all of us, expecting some new phenomenon and following the request by the table, were or pretended to be distracted. This is one of the funniest things during these sessions: the table commands with four raps: *"Converse!"* and we answer in chorus: "Fine ... so ... let us converse ... as ... you were saying ...." but hardly have we uttered these silly words when everybody falls back to a religious silence and our eyes, which momentarily had been wandering off, eagerly return to gaze at the *medium*. Eusapia took hold of my right forefinger, which more or less had the form of an electric switch, pressed it with her fingers, and all of a sudden a beam illuminated the room from inside the mediumistic cabinet, and an exclamation of joy came out of Eusapia's mouth.

It is easier to imagine than to describe the amazement of those who could not make sense of what had happened. I exclaimed: "Bravo; Bravo! Press it again, do it again." And the others: "Bravo, but what is it? What's the matter? What have you cooked up?" And I explained to them that the switch that was thrown on the table was connected to an electric lamp up on the cabinet wall. Eusapia, with one of her invisible hands, had searched and found the switch after it was carried away from the table. She had pressed it with the invisible hand while pressing my forefinger with the visible hand, and in so doing she had turned the light on, to everybody's amazement. This phenomenon also took place in crisscrossed direction, as I mentioned earlier.

Meanwhile, as always when Eusapia is successful, she repeated it several times. She repeatedly turned the lamp on, and since she did not know where it was located, she turned around towards the cabinet to look again. Every now and then the switch seemed to slip out of her touch. She looked for it, found it, and pressed it again. Everybody heard the switch being dragged on the floor during her attempts, as she seemed to be looking for it by the guidance of the cord. The light was repeatedly turned on and off four or five times. I asked Eusapia to leave the switch in peace, and pass on to something else, but she was amusing herself. She begged me to let her turn the light on once more, and then another time, until she finally stopped. One lighting lasted many seconds. It is worth noting that had it been one of us turning the bright light on unexpectedly in the obscure room, who knows what kind of cry of disdain and pain Palladino would have given out. Done by her, it made her feel pleased with herself and not offended by the light. It seemed as though before turning the light on, she already had an intuition of what was going to happen. Finally, the switch was thrown back on the table, and I said: "Let me press it without touching it." She tried, but in vain. "In that case" I added, "press it yourself while it is here on the table," but she failed.

Another phenomenon filled us with amazement. The switch was placed on the table. Eusapia said: "Look how it is moving!" We all fixed our gaze on the small object and we saw that it rose a few millimeters above the tabletop, oscillated and vibrated, as if invaded by an interior quiver. Eusapia's hands, held by Galeotti and me, were at least thirty centimeters away from the switch.

At a certain moment Eusapia appeared to be touching an object inside the mediumistic cabinet while she was making analogous movements on my right hand with her fingers. She asked me:

"What is it? ... I felt something soft, humid ... what is it?" At first I did not understand. I thought of the soft membrane of the bellows and told her so. But she was not persuaded and answered:

"No, no! It is something soft ... you feel it too," (as if I were able, the way she is, to provide sensitive limbs to touch objects far away). Then I remembered the mastic, and asked her not to damage it with her fingers, but to leave an impression of her face on it, like she had done at other times. The next day we found on the mastic very superficial marks of three fingertips, and three clear scratches like made by nails of small fingers.

I'll just say that if Palladino was cheating, what interest would she have in informing her custodians that at a given moment she was ready to execute a fraud or was already doing it? Indeed, since she frequently let it be known what she was prepared to do, is doing, or has just done, it could have no other effect than that of intensifying the attention and surveillance among participants. Whoever cheats doesn't say: "Pay attention, I am going to cheat." Rather, he is interested in operating silently and later finds pleasure in the amazement caused by the unexpected effects. At least this makes good sense, but I cannot predict what the sophistication and cleverness of stubborn disbelievers could find to oppose. We shall have a chance to discuss the hypothesis of fraud based on additional facts.

After having left the mastic, which seemed to have given her an unpleasant sensation, Palladino was now first trying to move the chair and then the metal plate containing the mastic. I told her that they were useless efforts since the chair was fastened to the walls of the cabinet, and the plate was tied to the chair. She was annoyed, but being now used to finding immobilized objects that she would have preferred to have fly up in the air, she left the chair in peace. This, by the way, proved that my predictions were correct when I claimed that if we want her mediumistic activity to be practiced on certain objects and instruments especially, it is necessary to immobilize all of those that Eusapia is more familiar with, and prefers to move, drag, and transport.

We had to keep insisting through the whole session to get her finally to play the tambourine and to set the metronome in motion. We finally heard scratching on the surface of the tambourine while Eusapia's nails made synchronous movements on the palm of my right hand. The tambourine was then thrown to the floor and played repeatedly. This time we obtained a beautiful trace of a melody which Eusapia produced with her invisible fingers. On the top left of Fig. 13 one can see groups of three vertical lines corresponding to a series of three beats on the membrane: ta, ta, ta...ta, ta, ta...I said: "Beat hard!" and then she started to press my right foot with her left foot. It is possible that a stronger pressure of her foot corresponded to the highest line on Figure 14. A tambourine stick was also placed in the cabinet, but Eusapia did not use it. She played with her hands and feet.

She then wanted us to watch a more complicated action. She beat in perfect synchrony the tambourine and the séance table with her invisible hands, while with her visible and tangible hands she made small strokes on Galeotti's and my own hands. Up 'til now we had observed the simultaneous occurrence of four

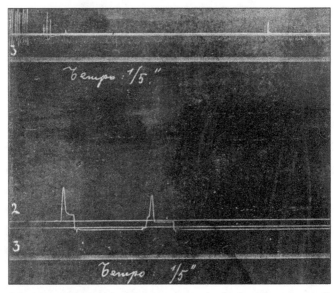

Figure 13. Fifth session. Top trace, signals obtained from the small drum; trace 3, time; trace 2, signals obtained from the bellows.

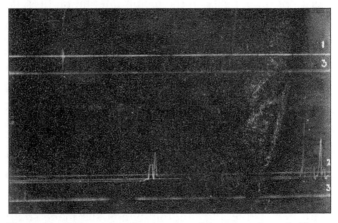

Figure 14. Fifth session. Continuation of the traces shown in Figure 13. Trace 1, signals obtained from the small drum; trace 3, time; trace 2, signals obtained from the bellows.

actions, two mediumistic and two bodily acts. But if one considers that the corporal limbs are four, and admits that each of them might be doubled, one might even observe eight simultaneous actions. We need to bear in mind, however, that for us it is practically impossible to carry out four simultaneous asymmetric actions with our four limbs.

The bellows connected to the mercury manometer was also pressed, and this time we obtained a much better trace of the pressures exerted on the membrane. But let me narrate in a more orderly fashion.

Eusapia was exploring and touching in the cabinet. By then I could sense the mediumistic exploration of her fingers from her pose and face, and in the barely detectable wormlike movements of her small fingers. She asked me: "What is this round thing...I feel something round..." "Which yields to pressure ..." I added. "Yes," Eusapia answered. "Press it, press it then, just like that, with your hand or also with your foot."

And I made her do the necessary movement to considerably raise the mercury column of the manometer.

In its own language the trace reported the number of times she pressed it, sometimes harder, sometimes lighter. I may add that at the same time I felt more or less heavy presses on my hand or foot.

What I have already hinted at but want to insist on now, is that with her invisible hands Eusapia felt form, consistency, cold and hot, hard and soft, humid and dry, exactly the same way she would feel by touching and feeling with her physical hands that were imprisoned in our own hands. She felt with the other hands, but perceived with the same brain and manifested her perceptions with the same vocal organs she was using during the peculiar conversation that characterized the late hours of every mediumistic session. At times such conversations seemed to be carried out by her, at other times by somebody else who was talking through her mouth, calling her "my daughter". Even while Eusapia appeared to be in a deep state of *trance*, she detected an unpleasant comment and immediately struck back. She did it sometimes with disdain, sometimes by laughing scornfully, or with unkind words revealing her offended self-respect. These were conversations during which good spiritualistic rules were imposed always to address our words to John King, the mysterious being who did everything taking place during the session. I complied with these rules only on some evenings, and never during the entire session, since I grew convinced that all mediumistic phenomena were due to the *medium*'s own activity (whatever nature it might have), be it conscious or unconscious.

Eusapia explored and touched with her mediumistic hands everything she could find in the cabinet. For this reason she had no need to try to inspect it beforehand. I was never convinced that she was also able to look inside the cabinet with 'mediumistic eyes.' Indeed, if she could have done this, she would not have run into so much trouble in finding the object she was asked to touch, and which she often found only after a long time and repeated searches. On the other hand, one observed materializations of arms and hands but also of heads. (I believe apparitions of feet have never been ascertained by any one yet.) The meaning of this last argument cannot be fully understood until I describe the way I represent to myself the determinism of mediumistic phenomena. I shall do this later on.

At a certain moment we heard a rhythmic beat, not on the floor, but on the tripod, and of a different sound from that of the tambourine. I interpreted it to be the tambourine stick beating on the wooden box covering one of the keys. But since my explanations did not seem to satisfy the sitters, in confirmation the stick was suddenly thrown on the séance table as if saying: "See? It is me who was beating." Some of us touched and observed it, and then it was taken away.

All of a sudden, without any warning from the *medium*, we heard a sharp blow on the séance table. I looked and touched it: one of the glasses had arrived on the table after having poured its copper sulfate solution on nearby people. Having touched my suit with my left hand, I found it wet, and complained about it to Eusapia, requesting her to no longer make these practical jokes since the glasses — I insisted — were not filled with harmless water but with liquids that leave stains.

Hardly had I finished my say, when one heard the special sound made by a liquid forcefully being poured out of a container on the floor. Soon thereafter the other glass, almost empty, was laid with a sharp blow on the table next to the first one.

How can we avoid expressing the idea that soon came to our mind that the *medium* had intentionally done all this? That after hearing that the liquid was dangerous, she had thrown the contents of the second glass to the floor before bringing it to the table, since she had previously believed that glasses were filled with just water? Because of these simple yet revealing facts, why not recognize the intimate connection existing between mediumistic phenomena and the *medium*'s consciousness, that is, their physiological determinism?

One thing is sure: it was not a being extraneous to the organism of the *medium* who produced the mediumistic phenomena. In fact, the *medium* was always aware of them, whether she expressed it or let it be guessed through the way phenomena occurred with respect to those attending their development.

Some drops of the second liquid were nevertheless left in the glass, and since they had been spilled on the table, the liquid reacted with the first liquid forming copper ferricyanide. A spot is still visible even today on the wood and on my handkerchief which I used for wiping the table dry and thus freeing hyperaesthetic Palladino from her annoyed sense of dampness.

Glasses did not break. They were placed upright on the table with a sharp blow. How did they get there? While speaking of this, let me remark that objects were seldom thrown. Usually, those brought onto the table reached it in an orderly way, and were then left in their place without a jerk. If they were thrown, they would overturn, roll across the table, and maybe end up on the floor. To the contrary, this almost never happened: objects reached a certain position on the table and remained there precisely as if placed by a hand. This hand could not be seen. Only at times was the object accompanied by the curtain, and then one had the impression that a hand behind the curtain, enveloped by it, grasped the object and carried it out of the mediumistic cabinet. It was not always like this. At other times an invisible hand did not carry the object to the table, but handed it out from behind the side of the curtain or through its middle opening. As stated before, whoever grabbed it, felt no resistance. Finally, at still other times, the curtain did not move at all, did not approach the table, and no hands or arms were coming out of the cabinet. Yet objects reached the table, but were not seen crossing the space even if they were of considerable dimensions.

Some more light was turned on. Galeotti brought the balance and the blackened cylinder to the séance table and placed the pen on the paper. I explained to Palladino what we wanted her to do: to lower the balance plate without touching it with her visible hands. The cylinder was set in motion and the pen drew a horizontal line of several rounds. A few seconds passed and we saw the left curtain advancing resolutely towards the table, as if pushed by a hidden hand from inside whose outline of fingers we distinctly saw. The curtain caught the balance plate and pressed it strongly. It then retracted and disappeared. We stopped the cylinder and noticed that the pen had written a vertical line on the blackened paper (badly, because the invisible hand had made the balance to oscillate a little). Eusapia's hands were in our custody!

Next day I decided to check what the balance index indicated when the plate had been pressed down and found out that the pressure on the plate was equivalent to a weight of 370 g. The two traces are reproduced in Figures 15 and 16, one made by the mediumistic hand, the other by my hand.

When the session was over, Scarpa, Jona, and Galeotti told me that Palladino had approached the balance, placed her hands by the sides of the plate, her fingertips facing the plate, and made the balance plate go up and down repeatedly by moving hands up and down. Scarpa assured me that he had heard a

Figure 15. Fifth session. The trace labeled abscissa shows the lowering of the plate of the letter-weighing balance accomplished by the mediumistic hand. Additional labeling: horizontal arrow, direction of the cylinder rotation; vertical arrow, direction of the lowering of the pen, hence of the plate of the letter-weighing balance.

Figure 16. Fifth session. Lowering of the plate of the letter-weighing balance made by Bottazzi's hand to determine the force needed to obtain the comparable signal made by the mediumistic hand which is shown in Figure 15. Additional labeling: top, session of May 3, 1907 it highlights the [unreadable] of the previous trace.

sound like nails rubbing metal, identical to what would have been produced had Palladino's fingers physically touched the balance plate.

I am not going to waste my time to tell the story of the hair Eusapia had used on another occasion to perform a similar experiment. The story is described in detail in a recent book by Flammarion.[5] It is certain that even if she was able to tear one hair, make a loop of it, and use it to lower the balance plate, the use of a hair cannot explain the degree of lowering recorded on the cylinder, nor the movements of the ebonite stick she produced on previous evenings, nor the strumming of the mandolin. It is hard to say why that evening of November 16, 1898, Eusapia felt the need to cheat her friends in Paris with her famous hair while only a few evenings earlier she had made the same experiment definitely without fraud (as affirmed by Flammarion).

What I can state here with certainty is that during our sessions many phenomena did not take place although eagerly awaited by us: impression of the face on mastic, levitation of the *medium* sitting on her chair, etc. Eusapia never tried to make them happen using fraudulent ways like that of the hair, and she was right in so doing. She should have realized that if just one of the simplest phenomena she repeated every evening was proved to be genuine, that phenomenon would be well worth all the rest, including the most extraordinary and marvelous ones.

Be that as it may, we were prepared to point out loudly any attempt of fraud at the very moment it could

[5]C. Flammarion, *Les forces naturelles inconnues*, pp. 270–271. Paris, 1907.

be detected. I cannot understand people who say: "I saw Palladino do something by using a hair, but did not rush to seize it from her, to grab at least a small piece to obtain indisputable evidence of fraud." I would do it in front of anybody and would keep that hair as a relic, in view of the great relevance of that discovery. Indeed, the famous 'Eusapian hair' mentioned by Flammarion seems to have been *seen* but not *taken*.

There was a lot of noise in the cabinet, creaking of wood, then a rap and a bump on the floor. It was unclear what had fallen. But Eusapia gave a sigh of relief, and soon one heard the hammering on the electric key. Then I understood. Being unable to reach the key in the wooden box, she had torn the box which was fastened to the underlying shelf with three screws and, victorious, had started to hammer the key furiously (Fig. 17). I soon calmed her down by saying: "Thank you, Eusapia, but this was not what I wanted. You were supposed to beat the key without breaking the box."

The trace corresponding to the beats on the key is very important.

Later on, the wooden box thrown on the floor was offered to Prof. De Amicis through the central opening of the curtains, and he placed it on the table.

Eusapia said: "Attention!" and one heard synchronous beats on the key and on the séance table. Eusapia said once more: "Attention!" And one heard

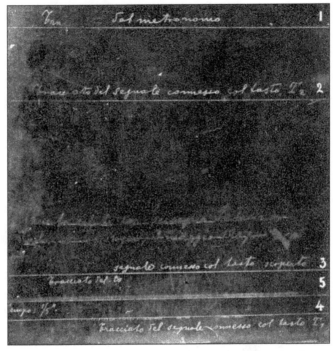

Figure 17. Fifth session. Traces 1 to 4 were obtained from the electric metronome and from the T2, T3, and T1 keys, respectively. Only trace 4 derived from the T1 key showed groups of frequent beats and beats lasting several fifths of a second (see text for explanations). Trace 5, time. Additional labeling: trace 1, metronome trace; trace 2, trace of signal connected with the T2 key; trace, 3, trace of signal connected with the not enclosed key; trace 4, trace of signal connected with the T1 key; trace 5, time.

synchronous beats on the table and on the tambourine, on the table, and on the key in alternate sequence.

Although one was used to these phenomena by then, we were always deeply impressed. Consider this: when Eusapia said "Attention!" everyone held his breath and looked at her. There was a profound silence in the room. Eusapia herself was motionless, as if listening to the beats. On the other side of the curtains inside the dark cabinet one was hearing the beats on the electric key clear and hard, perfectly synchronous with the beats either on the table in front of us or on the tambourine on the floor. All this happened without the arms and hands of the *medium* making any attempt to penetrate into the cabinet, while seven alert and attentive participants had their eyes fixed on her. Only her fingers pressed rhythmically in a barely audible way on our hands, as if providing the rhythm to the inside beats.

It was a simple phenomenon, yet marvelous and astounding! It was simple, but who can explain it? Who was beating there? And how come beats from inside were synchronous with the beats here and the imperceptible presses of the *medium*'s fingers? This synchrony forced us to admit that mediumistic beats and presses by Eusapia's fingers, or rather movements determining both of them, had a common point of origin. Quite plausibly this is the brain, the will of Eusapia. I will never get tired of repeating it.

The beating on the key continued on and off for a long time, but the signs on the trace were not as numerous (Fig. 17). The next morning we discovered that one of the cords connecting the key to the signal was torn out near the key. It is impossible to say when and how this had happened.

Meanwhile Scarpa had placed himself between Palladino and me. He kept the mediumistic chain with his left hand and maintained his right hand and arm almost continuously, with Eusapia's consent, around Eusapia's shoulders. She was leaning on his arm, and this helped him to exert better surveillance and to feel the movements of her shoulder muscles that Eusapia made in synchrony with mediumistic phenomena taking place inside or outside the mediumistic cabinet. At a certain moment, however, while Scarpa's head was almost touching the curtain, he felt his hair seized and pulled three times so strongly that he screamed out in pain. He assured us that some hair was torn off. Eusapia, after having kindly invited him to her side, had taken vengeance over Scarpa's zest of surveillance and control. In fact, for the entire evening Eusapia had been unable to detain herself from expressing her resentment for his leaving the chain, approaching the curtain, taking the mastic plate, seeing if there were any marks, etc. Finally Eusapia said: "That one" (Scarpa) "annoys me. Sit down, go to your place, go away!"

In time they became friends and, as mentioned, she wanted him near her, but mainly to pull his leg.

While Scarpa was so close to Palladino, he had several occasions to cast a look into the mediumistic cabinet and behind her back. He then thought that he saw something resembling stumps, outlines of limbs budding out of the *medium*'s trunk which moved indistinctly and then disappeared.

But I will return to this when reporting what I saw during the seventh session.

It is unnecessary to say that during a session filled with phenomena like these, touches and kisses were numerous. As soon as Cardarelli moved to replace Galeotti, he was greeted by touches and pulling of his chair and left arm. He asked for a kiss and soon the curtain swelled out with the outline of a human profile, approached his cheek, and one heard a kiss being smacked, while Eusapia made the act of kissing.

I was also touched in many parts of my body. One of these little touches I will never forget because it was repeated many times. I felt three fingers of a hand squeezing my right knee quite hard.

Galeotti was pulled by the sleeve of his jacket towards the cabinet, and clearly saw the hand that was pulling him.

Eusapia asked engineer Jona to climb on the séance table and to remain there on his knees. I pointed out that the table was rather fragile. All the same Jona, who weighs about 78 kg, climbed up with his face turned towards Palladino. The curtain became restless, moved forward, swirled and approached Jona's head. I heard something like a rubbing where the curtain was touching Jona's head. We asked him: "What did you feel?" And he answered: "I definitely felt a hand caressing my beard."

The curtain returned back to its place. The table with Jona on top levitated a few centimeters above the floor, especially on Eusapia's side, while her knees made very clear efforts as if to lift something up. I had placed my right hand on her knees, and my left hand held her left hand.

Cardarelli now felt something approaching his forehead until touching it. "Is it a hand?" "No." Palladino asked: "Did you feel a contact with the hair?" At first Cardarelli could not distinguish it. We asked Eusapia: "Is it hair or beard?" "Hair," she said. "Yes, hair," added Cardarelli.

Maybe Eusapia was touching Cardarelli's head with her *other* head to make him feel the contact with hair, the same way she previously caressed Jona with her *other* hand.

But the mediumistic head was not seen. It was like the hand earlier behind the curtain on which we *very clearly* could see its outline.

We have an additional mystery here! Why do mediumistic hands and heads appear nude sometimes (like during the seventh session), and *materialize* up to the point of becoming visible, or both visible and tangible, while at other times they prefer to remain hidden behind the curtains like it happened that evening? And in this second case, if the curtain would

magically disappear, could we see the hand or the
head making the outline? Definitely the outline on
the curtain was not only visible, but also tangible. It
showed resistance and consistency, as if behind the
curtain there really existed a head similar to ours.
But *materialization* is unlikely to occur to the same
degree in the two cases. Between black hands and
heads clearly outlined by the curtain, hands and heads
advancing as if enveloped by the curtain, and hands
and heads presenting themselves nude, of dull color
as human skin, bony and muscular, warm or with
temperature similar to ours, between these three kinds
of materializations there must be some difference,
perhaps not a superficial difference, but we cannot
say what it is.

We cannot forget apparitions that failed. While
Eusapia was at the top of her mediumistic excite-
ment, she cried out again: "Attention!" We saw the
right curtain move to the left and protrude into the
cabinet to an extent not seen before, which left almost
half of the cabinet completely open. Eusapia urged:
"Attention ... look at the figure ... " "What figure?"
"That of a woman!" We all fixed our eyes on the sides
of the cabinet sides, then up and down. Nothing, there
was nothing to be seen!

This was not the first time Eusapia announced
a phenomenon nobody was able to detect. But this
time we were really disappointed. The sight of the

announced figure would have been the climax of the session. Why didn't we see anything? Was Eusapia trying to make a fool of us, or did she lack the sufficient force to shape up the figure, at least visible if not tangible, that certainly was molded in her psyche?

A mystery!

After the session we noticed that the front side of the metal box containing one of the keys had been bent a little, as if pressed hard by a hand. The uncovered key had not been touched, nor the metronome.

It is noteworthy that after every session Palladino had considerable hyperalgesia (exaggerated sensitivity to pain) on her hands, especially on their back side. She said it felt like burning, as if her hands had been immersed in lye for a long time. In fact, her hands were always red and hot, and the subcutaneous veins appeared full of blood.

From this evening on we collected Palladino's urine immediately before and after the session to compare them. This time the second urine was lost by mistake. I shall report the results of urine collected before the session:

Urine quantity: cm^3 120;
Specific weight (+15°):   1034;
Acid reaction (quite intense);
Appearance clear;
Yellow amber color (Vogel II tab.);
Abundant sediment (after 12 hours).

Examination of decanted urine:

Albumin: 2 g per thousand;

Glucose absent;

Total nitrogen (in albumin-free urine by means of asaprol acid solution): 12.105 g per thousand.

Alkaline and earthy phosphates in excess.

Microscopic examination of the sediment:

Numerous mucus pus particles;

Cells of the low urogenital tract.

Few red blood cells;

Uric concretions.

X. Sixth Session (May 6, 1907).

At 21:00, barometric pressure (Capodimonte Observatory) = 752.4; T = 16.4°C. Relative humidity of the atmosphere: 72%.

Present were Profs. Cardarelli, Galeotti, Pansini, Scarpa, De Amicis, and Bottazzi. Prof. Lombardi was back, who substituted for engineer Jona. Also present was lawyer N. Minutillo, who remained outside the mediumistic chain for most of the session.

The weather was hot and humid, sultry, oppressive. The sirocco wind was blowing. Eusapia seemed to be in a good mood. The return of Lombardi and Minutillo made no impression on her. At first, I remained outside the chain. Eusapia's hands were in custody of Cardarelli on the left and De Amicis on the right, followed by Scarpa, Galeotti, Lombardi, and Pansini. Minutillo was sitting on the couch. I took notes while sitting between Lombardi and Galeotti.

The session started at 21:15, and ended at midnight.

Several changes had been made in the mediumistic cabinet. Since the session was supposed to be the last one, and we were now well convinced of the reality of the observed phenomena, we decided to leave Eusapia free to play, and had not immobilized a new walnut table brought into the cabinet. We placed on it, in the back, the instrument to blacken the cylinders with smoke along with a smoked cylinder, the trumpet, and the metronome; in front from left to right, an electric key uncovered and fastened to the table with screws, two Erlenmeyer flasks filled up to three quarters of their capacity, one with a potassium ferrocyanide solution and the other one with ferric chloride, a wire-mesh cage containing a secured telegraph key, two half-filled glasses, one containing a copper sulfate solution, the other one a potassium ferrocyanide solution, the usual tambourine connected to the mercury manometer and the two sticks, and the bellows connected to the Marey kettledrum. Other objects were put here and there without any specific order.

The electric lamp from the previous session was left in the left corner, but the pressure switch was hung on a nail on the left wall of the cabinet. The switch was never pressed despite our repeated requests to Eusapia, perhaps because it was beyond the sphere of mediumistic action. Hence, the lamp was never lit.

The first phenomenon worth mentioning was that the chair on Eusapia's right side with a plate of mastic on top started to move, and step by step was carried forward. At a certain moment the plate was thrown on the floor (after the session, a deep mark of the edge of the chair was found on the mastic). I was convinced, and succeeded in convincing the others that, as in the previous session, the plate did not fall by sliding but was overturned and thrown to the floor, perhaps to make the chair lighter. The enameled metal plate full of mastic had always been ill treated by Eusapia, nobody knows why.

Meanwhile, the lightened chair continued to approach the table. It finally rose up and came in sight between the curtains with its back inclined forward, behind and above Palladino's head. I forgot to say that the chair was completely covered by the left curtain in its original position, and could thus be considered to be inside the cabinet. In the meantime I had slipped momentarily between Cardarelli and the *medium* to see better. Since someone could get hurt if the chair fell, I hurried to grab the chair and felt no resistance. I asked Eusapia if I could put it on the floor; she answered "yes," and I placed it in the right hand corner behind Cardarelli. I then asked if I could sit on it; Eusapia gave me a signal with her head meaning yes. So, I started moving the chair a little towards the wall and sat down on it between Cardarelli and Palladino, but in doing it I felt strong resistance. At first I believed that the chair could not be moved because some obstacle was somehow preventing it, but then looking down I realized that the chair was free, and still could not be moved.

The sensation I had while pulling it resembled that of its feet being secured to the floor with strong elastic bands, or held by a robust arm making antagonistic movements to mine. A few minutes later, turning to John, I finally said that if he wanted me to sit on the chair, he must let the chair go. He complied, and I sat down.

During the journey of the chair, one glass fell to the floor and broke into pieces. I said that the chair had thrown it down when passing by. Eusapia vigorously replied: "No!" "All right, so it must have been me," I added. "I knocked it down when grabbing the chair sticking out above Eusapia's head." Naturally, it was difficult to know who was right.

The session became long-winded, and Galeotti claimed that my presence in that corner was interfering with mediumistic activity. Nonetheless, when questioned, the table repeatedly answered: *"No!"* And I remained there.

I was touched on my right ankle, arm, and hip (and I was out of the chain). On the other hand, Cardarelli was never touched and said I shielded him. He too wanted me to leave my post.

De Amicis was touched several times. He asked to be kissed. The curtain advanced toward him twice, as if pushed by a face hiding behind, approached his face, and one heard the smack of a kiss. De Amicis wanted to know who kissed him and he begged the table to answer with the usual raps. But the replies were inconsistent. Since we were losing a lot of time, I grumbled and asked Eusapia to stop.

Suddenly the table inside the mediumistic cabinet started to move. As predicted, this produced a real disaster. While moving, the table positioned itself in such a way as to oscillate on two of its four legs, and so it started dancing. The trumpet fell, the drum was thrown to the floor, and the metronome and the keys were displaced. In vain I prayed John to leave the table in peace and rather put in action the instruments above. He liked that silly dance and kept going with it.

Finally the table stopped, and we started to hear the uncovered key being beaten. I immediately picked up another spring key identical to that being acted upon in the mediumistic cabinet, and put it on the séance table in front of Palladino.

The two keys (the outside one through two long electric cords) were connected to two Desprez signals in the adjacent room. Their pens were placed on the cylinder on the same vertical line, one on top of the other.

I explained to Palladino what we expected from her. "Look," I said. "There is a pair of keys: one is inside the cabinet, the other one is this one. You need to press this one with your visible hand, and the other one like you did just now but in such a way that the pressing takes place simultaneously. Have you understood?" "Yes," she replied.

She collected the curtain with her left hand, and started to press the outside key in front of our eyes with two fingers (index and middle finger). All participants heard that each outside beat corresponded to the beat on the key inside the mediumistic cabinet. This sensation was distinctly clear as the two keys did not produce the same sound although they had the same shape.

Palladino was inclined forward over the table, her face intently absorbed in the movements she was making with her left hand. That hand was in contact with my right hand and Cardarelli's right hand, while Eusapia's right hand was in custody of Prof. De Amicis. Since the right curtain was drawn over the table and was wrapped to a great extent around Eusapia's left arm and hand, the mediumistic cabinet was only half-covered, and I could cast a searching eye inside it several times. But nothing in the least was revealed that could have elicited the suspicion of a fraud.

The traces reproduced in Figures 18, 19, and 20 show groups of synchronous beats (of 8 or 11) and isolated beats on both the outside and inside keys. Isolated beats corresponded partly to those made by Eusapia while she was learning the task, partly to those preceding the experiment. As to the groups where one can establish synchronism of beats in the Figures, one could count two groups in the traces 1 and 2 of Figure 18, two in the traces of Figure 19, two or three in the traces of Figure 20. Unfortunately, the signaling pens did not write properly. This was not my fault but John's, who shook the table in the

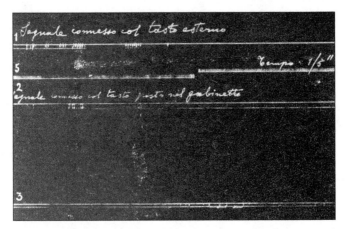

Figure 18. Sixth session. Trace 1, signals obtained from the key placed on the séance table; trace 2, signals obtained from the key placed inside the mediumistic cabinet; trace 3, signals obtained from the metronome; trace 5, time. Additional labeling: trace 1, signal connected with the external key; trace 2, signal connected with the key placed in the cabinet; trace 5, time.

mediumistic cabinet at the beginning of the session, and moved the internal key by pulling its cords, producing a shifting of signals and displacing them a bit from the cylinder surface. Nevertheless, if the traces are not beautiful, they were still demonstrative. What was shown in an irrefutable way was that the two keys were beaten several times in perfect synchrony. The outside key was beaten with Eusapia's left hand and the inside one with the other hand, which for Eusapia would have been that of her father, John King, for a convinced spiritualist that of a materialized spirit (?!), and for me neither one, despite my not being capable of saying what it was.

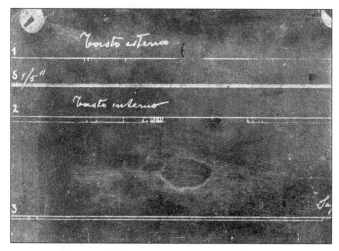

Figure 19. Sixth session. Continuation of the traces 1, 2, 3, and 5 shown in Figure 18. Additional labeling: trace 1, external key; trace 2, internal key.

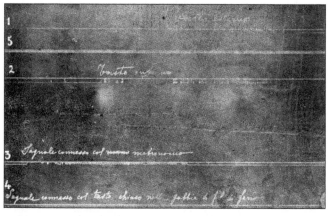

Figure 20. Sixth session. Continuation of the traces 1, 2, 3, and 5 shown in Figure 19. Trace 4, trace derived from the key enclosed in the wire cage. Additional labeling: trace 1, external key; trace 2, internal key; trace 3, Signal connected with the metronome; trace 4, Signal connected with the key enclosed in the wire mesh cage.

We told Palladino that on the cabinet table there
were two small flasks filled with liquid, and that we
wanted her to pour one liquid over the other (one of
the two glasses had fallen to the floor, and so we could
not ask her to mix their liquids). Meanwhile I had my
right arm around Eusapia's back, seemingly to offer
support, but in reality to keep better control over her
arms, and to feel her movements. We heard from the
cabinet slight sounds of bottles touching each other,
and soon thereafter the characteristic noise made by
a liquid being poured from a certain height, first onto
another liquid, then to the floor. It is unnecessary to
mention that Palladino's arms remained in their place.
I alone felt, a few seconds before the sound of bottles
touching each other was heard, lively fibrillatory movements in the muscles of her right shoulder. Meanwhile,
she had remained immobile and appeared absorbed,
certainly in the interior preparation of the phenomenon
which followed.

As soon as I heard the liquid being poured to the
floor, I hurried to tell Eusapia: "Pay attention, you are
pouring it to the floor. You should instead pour it into
the bottle next to it." But the liquid kept falling down
and spreading all over the floor to the entrance of the
mediumistic cabinet and under Palladino's dress. Then
the empty bottle was brought to the séance table in the
usual manner. Since some drops of the liquid had still
remained, the following day I made proper analyses

and found that it was the bottle containing the potassium ferrocyanide solution. Thinking that the experiment had failed, and that the *medium* had poured one solution entirely to the floor rather than into the other liquid, we started to make unkind comments on Eusapia's ineptitude. But a few minutes later the other bottle was suddenly and violently thrown to the middle of the room where it broke into pieces leaving a large radial stain on the floor

"It is John avenging our comments," I said.

Being persuaded that the experiment had failed, that evening we did not pay much attention to anything else other than what already had happened. But the next day, after having carefully examined the battlefield, I found a large bluish stain on the floor in the middle of the room right where the pieces of the second bottle were, and additional spots of the same color on the table inside. Evidently, the two liquids had been mixed before the second bottle was thrown out of the cabinet, since otherwise the color of the stain could not have been Prussian blue. As a result, the spilling of the liquid to the floor had to be otherwise explained.

I stated that the two flasks had been filled up to three quarters of their capacity. The first liquid was poured into the second one, and when the second flask was full, the rest of the liquid had to go to the floor. It was sheer luck that the second bottle was thrown far away from the cabinet, for had it fallen on the same

spot where the liquid was spilled at first, there would
have been no way of deciding whether the mixing of
the liquids had taken place in the bottles or on the
floor, irrespective of the blue spot we found.

The barium platinum-cyanide plate was moved out of
the cabinet and brought to the séance table. In complete
darkness we asked Eusapia to put her hands above it
and approach it with her head. Although these attempts
were repeated, we never saw the plate become luminous.
However, Palladino did not want it to be removed.

At a certain moment Eusapia said in a clear voice:
"I touched the blackened cylinder, look at my fingers."

She stretched out at first one hand then the other
toward us. We carefully examined her fingers, but
there was no trace of black smoke. Yet, on the cylinder,
there were very clear marks of small fingertips like
those of Eusapia.

One could distinguish lines of skin on the white
marks. Judged by their form it seemed that the fingers
both touched and scraped the paper. Perhaps these
short scrapings corresponded to the efforts made by a
hand trying to make the cylinder rotate. Whatever that
may be, the cylinder did rotate at least twice around
its axis because two horizontal lines were drawn on
the blackened paper by the pen touching the cylinder.
The rotation took place in the opposite direction of
the usual one because the point of the pen (made of

a flexible sheet of horn) was bent, perhaps where the paper had been rough, and instead of writing two thin lines it drew two broad white stripes.

Despite the fact that the drum and the Marey kettle-drum were in front of the blackened cylinder, this time they were not even touched.

We insisted several times on her pressing the key inside the wire mesh cage. I gave Eusapia all necessary explanations. I said: "It is no use for you to strain yourself trying to take off the cover of the cage since it is firmly secured with string. It is also of no use to hit the sides of the cage because the key inside cannot be put into action that way. If you cannot do it in some other way, try at least to put a finger through the net and press the key."

But all attempts were in vain. We clearly heard the scratching and hitting on the sides of the cage but that hand could not penetrate into the cage. The key was not touched and the respective trace of the Desprez signal bore no marks.

As a result, the experiment we considered so important gave negative results. The invisible hand operating in the mediumistic cabinet, like our hands, was incapable of penetrating through the screen. Even a wire mesh with large openings was sufficient to prevent it from going through. How can one maintain that that hand is, so to say, a spiritual, an immaterial hand?

Eusapia said to me: "Take it, take it!" "What is it?"

I got up, and looked behind her into the cabinet, opening the curtains. The cage was moving forward; it was already at the height of Eusapia's head but could not reach the séance table because the electric cords connected to the key were entangled. I grabbed the cage, untangled the cords, and brought it to the table. I then asked Eusapia to examine it, and showed her the inside key. I took the cage back to the cabinet and asked Eusapia to activate the key in a mediumistic way. We waited quite a while but nothing happened!

On the floor there were a flower vase and the mandolin. The vase was put down, possibly when the table was displaced. The mandolin was not played.

The metronome was set in motion. In addition to rhythmic oscillations of the rod shown in the lower trace of Figure 20, I clearly heard isolated beats which cannot occur unless the rod is manually moved to the right or to the left, regardless of the charge of the metronome. Not everybody recognized these isolated beats, because the respective acoustic sensations could easily be produced by other means. But I knew the sound of the metronome quite well, and kept insisting that those sounds corresponded to oscillations of the rod of the metronome. "Then let's find out who is right," we concluded.

In addition to the rhythmic series of signals shown in Figure 20, the traces also showed isolated and irregular signals like those in Figures 18 and 19.

So I was not wrong. The rod of the metronome had undoubtedly been moved as if a hand had pushed it left and right. It could be doubted whether the shock that set the metronome in rhythmic motion (Fig. 20) was produced by a mediumistic hand. It could have been attributed to one of the strongest displacements of the table. But the isolated beats I heard while the table remained immobile could only have been made by a hand.

If I linger on this particular detail, it is because the metronome was never absent from among the objects placed in the mediumistic cabinet during previous sessions, but this was the first time it was set in motion irrespective of the shocks to the table or the charge on the spring. This is a fact of non-negligible value.

The metronome was carried to the séance table, put in front of Eusapia, and she was asked to move the rod without touching it. She tried it, but unsuccessfully. Scarpa showed how this could be done and made three or four beats himself (they have to be removed from those recorded in the trace despite our not knowing which was which). No results, nothing!

At this point the session could have been called to an end. Eusapia was tired. Nevertheless we tried to perform another experiment. The balance and a blackened cylinder were brought to the séance table, and Palladino was requested to lower the plate in a mediumistic way. She tried it but did not succeed.

Prof. Lombardi asked many times that the flask
on the table be moved, displaced, or even brought
back to the cabinet, but in vain. One could see that
Eusapia wished to satisfy his desire but was unable
to do it. Two or three times the curtain threw itself on
the table and enveloped the flask which did not move
one millimeter. A peculiar show! We all, including
the *medium*, wanted very much for the phenomenon to
take place and for Prof. Lombardi to be satisfied. The
curtain moved, advanced, reached to lick the flask or
wrap itself around it. At this point, an insurmountable
obstacle seemed to inhibit the completion of the phenomenon. The action desired by the *medium*, barely
initiated by the wrapping of the curtain, stopped and
Eusapia let out a sigh of anguish and weariness. Why
was all this happening? The unanimous will of the sitters and the *medium* was obvious, yet the very simple
phenomenon repeated earlier with other objects and in
many other occasions did not take place. Finally Prof.
Lombardi took Prof. Cardarelli's place, who had to go
home as he was not feeling too well due to the weather.
Under the new conditions, another phenomenon took
place under his eyes and guarding hand. It was just
as simple, but for this reason even more worth noting.
More light had been turned on since the session had
already been considered terminated, and someone
had already gotten up. Suddenly, the same chair I had
placed in the right corner started to move all by itself,

scraping its feet on the floor. We looked: Eusapia's feet were under the table, and her hands were about a meter away. Lombardi grabbed the back of the chair and pulled it. He felt resistance, as if someone was holding it from the other side. The chair kept moving as if to wriggle itself free from his hand, and it finally stopped.

As I said, it was a phenomenon of minor importance, but I was also happy that it had happened because in the two sessions attended by Prof. Lombardi, which were the least important ones (the first and the sixth), he was the least favored by Palladino's mediumistic activity.

Next morning, looking at what we called our battlefield, we found that the table inside the mediumistic cabinet had been moved, that the chair was no longer in its place, and the plate of mastic was on the floor. The cage was on the séance table, and the two spring keys which were synchronously beaten were on their tables. In between the two tables a large stain was on the floor, which had been produced by the liquid thrown on the floor.

Palladino's urine was collected and examined before and after the session.

A) Urine collected immediately before the session:

Quantity: cm³ 60;

Specific weight (+15°C): 1022;

Reaction: very acid;

Appearance: clear;

Color: amber-yellow
(Vogel II tab.);

Kept about 18 hours in a glass, the urine presented an abundant sediment.

Examination of the decanted urine.

Lowering of the freezing point (Δ) = 1°.240

Electric conductivity (K 19°C) = 150×10^{-4}

Albumin total: 1.25 g per thousand;

Nitrogen total (from dealbuminated urine):
9.53 g per thousand;

Small amount of glucose present.

Alkaline and earthly phosphates in excess.

Indican in excess.

Microscopic examination of the sediment.

Many mucus pus particles;

Cells of the low urogenital system;

Several uric acid crystals;

Few red blood cells;

Few cylinder-like particles.

B) Urine collected immediately after the session.
   Specific weight (+15°C): 1023;
   Quantity: cm³ 130;
   Reaction: very acid;
   Appearance: clear;
   Color: amber-yellow,
                          a little darker
                          (Vogel III tab.).
Abundant sediment after 18 hours.

Examination of the decanted urine.
   Lowering of the freezing point (Δ) = 1°.540;
   Electric conductivity (K19°C) = 177×10^{-4};
   Albumin total = 2 g per thousand;
   Nitrogen total from dealbumined urine:
      11.28 per thousand
   Presence of glucose;
   Alkaline and earthly phosphates in excess;
   Indican in excess.

Microscopic examination of the sediment.
   Results identical to the previous ones.

Comparison of the two samples of urine showed that the one taken after the session was considerably more concentrated. It had a higher specific weight, higher osmotic pressure and electric conductivity. Total nitrogen and albumin were also increased.

Kidneys seemed to produce more concentrated urine during the sessions. Despite the presence of albumin and sugar, values of osmotic pressure and electric conductivity of the urine differed little or not at all from the normal levels. Microscopic examination never showed the presence of kidney cells nor cylinders. This was a strange case of chronic albuminuria without definite signs of nephritis.

The observation of strong urine acidity and abundant content in uric acid was remarkable. Some uric acid crystals were already present shortly after urine was collected. Their number increased enormously, and the layer they formed with time became macroscopically visible while the urine remained acid. Eusapia was undoubtedly a subject of clearly arthritic character, a uricemic person.

XI. Seventh Session (May 11, 1907).

At 21:00 the barometric pressure at the Capodimonte Observatory = 753.9; T = 17.2°C. Relative atmospheric humidity = 76%.

This session was held on behalf of Mr. H. B. (this gentleman expressed in a letter to me his wish to remain anonymous). He was present together with his wife, as well as Prof. Galeotti, Doctor Pasquale Poso, assistant of the Royal Obstetrical Clinic of Naples, and I. Mr. B. is a convinced spiritualist, has attended numerous mediumistic sessions in France, England, and elsewhere. Passing through Naples with his wife, and having learnt that the famous *medium* E. Palladino was here, he did not want to miss the opportunity of having a session especially held for him. Eusapia preferred to hold the session in the same place as the other six sessions, and in our company.

A relevant modification had been made in the mediumistic cabinet. As I considered the one we had used up 'til now to be too small, I had it enlarged by extending a metal wire from its upper left corner to the upper left corner of the door at the right of the mediumistic cabinet. The two curtains were attached by rings to this wire. As a result, the new mediumistic cabinet was open on top.

The heavy table used in the first session was placed in the old mediumistic cabinet. Since it could be moved, I decided to immobilize it with a robust wooden pole fastened to the two walls and nailed to the legs of the table. On the upper shelf of the table there were the cage with the key inside, two Erlenmeyer flasks filled with the familiar solutions of potassium ferrocyanide and ferric chloride, one of the two spring keys, a small Gaiffe electro-magnetic machine which had been modified to be operated as an electric switch (see later), a candle, and matches.

On the lower shelf there were a bottle full of water and an empty glass, a beautiful bunch of roses in a high glass filled with water, and the trumpet.

On the right, outside the old cabinet, we had a stool with a wooden board on top and on it a loaf of soft statuary clay. Near the stool there was a chair with another wooden board carrying another bigger loaf of glazier mastic. Since we had never succeeded in obtaining the desired marks, presumably due to Eusapia's dislike of metal plates, I decided to place the clay and the mastic on a wooden surface.

The other spring key, similar to the one mentioned previously, was on a chair outside the cabinet, ready to be brought to the séance table at the right moment.

Eusapia came at 21:00 sharp accompanied by Mr. and Mrs. B. After presentations and courtesies, we formed the chain and started the session. We were six, Eusapia included. I assumed custody of her left hand, Mrs. B. was in front of me and had in custody her right hand (Mrs. B had also participated in other mediumistic sessions). On my left side was Dr. Poso, to the right of Mrs. B. was Prof. Galeotti, and opposite Eusapia sat Mr. B.

Apart from the movements and levitations of the table, we waited in vain more than half an hour for some phenomenon. During this time Dr. Poso's behavior towards Palladino was frankly irritating; his head was lowered and stretched out low over the table, his eyes fixed, almost stiffened on her eyes, his attitude resembling that of a tragic inquisitor. In vain we told him that one could keep the most meticulous watch without assuming such a tragic attitude, that it was useless to stare so insistently at Eusapia's face since it could not be presumed that she was performing her wonderful fraud just with her head. Palladino was visibly annoyed and so was I, thinking that the unexpected session in which I had put such great hopes might end in failure.

Fortunately, Poso changed his attitude after the first phenomena, and in addition Mr. and Mrs. B. seemed to exert a very effective stimulus on Eusapia's mediumistic activity, to the point of neutralizing and surmounting Dr. Poso's contrary influence.

The right curtain started to get restless, and a little later the chair with the mastic started to move. We recommended to Eusapia not to throw it to the floor but to fulfill our desire to see the mark of a human face on mastic. She answered yes, but did not do anything. After advancing quite a bit and approaching me almost to the point of touching me, the chair was left in peace.

The left curtain started to move forward, and Mrs. B. was repeatedly touched, tapped on her shoulder by an open hand so loudly that we all heard the strokes. Twice, as I stood in front of this lady, I saw the curtain with a distinct profile of fingers approach her cheeks, and she claimed that her ear was pulled.

Above Palladino's head between the curtains something bright appeared. It was hard to understand what it was. One of us stretched his arm to touch it but was too late. A sound was heard; it was one of the flasks that was offered but not grabbed, crashing to the floor and breaking into pieces. I recommended to Eusapia not to soil Mr. B's dress, and informed her that the flasks contained harmful liquids.

The invisible hands came to my side. I felt touched in many parts of my body, and felt blows on my chair. At a certain moment my chair was seized by its back (I distinctly felt on my back the fingers grabbing it), and was pulled backwards step by step towards the inside of the mediumistic cabinet. The chair crawled heavily on the floor describing an arc of a circle whose center was approximately Palladino's body. Let me point out that I weigh eighty nine kilograms and together with the chair, which weighs about four kilograms, the total is ninety three kilograms.

Next day, I decided to check if one of my assistants, a young and robust man, was capable of moving me sitting on the same chair. He had to use both arms to drag me a few centimeters, confessing he had to use all his strength!

"What then," I said, "do you want to carry me into the cabinet?"

"No" answered Eusapia (or rather John through Eusapia's mouth, according to Mr. B.). I went back to my place. The chair had been moved about forty centimeters.

We begged John several times to give Dr. Poso a direct proof of his presence. I took Poso's hand and approached it to the curtain, hoping his hand to be grabbed from inside the cabinet the way it had happened several times to other people during previous sessions. But the curtain remained immobile. No use to insist. John has his ill wills, likes, and dislikes. I jokingly said that John's hands manifest positive or negative tropism through their movements according to who happens to be present. In this particular case it seemed that an insurmountable barrier kept them separated from Doctor Poso's body.

There were many interesting cases of objects brought over.

At first, the glass with the bunch of roses appeared between curtains above Eusapia's head. I took it and

put it on the table, while not a drop of water was
spilled. Then came the candle, followed a moment
later by the faithful box of matches. The second flask
peeped out, and Eusapia warned us: "Pay attention,
this one could dye!"

It was the flask with ferric chloride, and not a drop
was spilled out of that one either.

Eusapia touched the clay with her mediumistic
hands and complained about the unpleasant sensation
of softness. Suddenly and very noisily, the wooden
board with clay on top was thrown from above (how
did it get there?) onto the séance table, and the clay
stack on its surface. Good-bye to my hope of imprints
on the clay, if there ever were any.

The tambourine sticks were violently thrown on the
séance table, and they ended up on the floor.

Finally the tambourine itself appeared. Galeotti
tried to take it, but the tambourine retreated, reappeared, and retreated again.

I have made a list rather than a description of this
sequence of marvelous phenomena not only for the
sake of brevity, but also because they took place with
velocity and precision like never before. But I need
to go back to two of them because they were the most
important ones.

The first one I shall call the episode of the roses.

I have mentioned that the vase with the bunch of
roses, presented from between the curtains above

Palladino's head, was received by me and placed in front of us. At some point, the left curtain moved towards the séance table, and a clearly recognizable hand behind it seized the bunch, threw it mockingly against Doctor Poso's outstretched face, and took away the glass filled with water. Now the scene of roses started, and the actor was still the mysterious hand covered by the curtain. It offered one rose to Mrs. B., placing it under her nose. Then it offered one to me, while Eusapia said in disguised voice, as when she speaks on behalf of John: "To my daughter's friend." Everybody was amazed! What did these obscure words mean? I put the rose on my buttonhole and asked: "Who is the friend of your daughter? Who is your daughter?"

My ignorance irritated Eusapia. At last Galeotti understood and explained: "It was John who was talking. Eusapia is his daughter, and his daughter's friend is your wife." And so the mystery was solved. John was kindly offering me a rose to be given to my wife.

"John, put a rose in Mrs. B.'s hair." We heard rustling on the floor, like hands searching the ground, and flowers being dragged. Then the curtain approached the lady's head, and placed one rose in her hair.

"John," Galeotti said, "give a rose to me too." The same curtain movements took place. A rose was picked up from the floor (some had fallen there, I couldn't say exactly when. Who knows why those on the table were not offered?) and was kindly offered to him.

"John, give a rose also to Doctor Poso."

That evening we were directly talking with John himself. The presence of a mysterious being behind the curtains was continuously felt, almost in contact with us, among us!

An absolute stillness of the curtain, a perfect silence, the mysterious being appeared to have become paralyzed by merely hearing the name of Poso.

A brief comment. A person sitting in Palladino's place, unless being a pithecanthropus with arms long enough to touch the floor and pick up a rose, would have to bend his body considerably to touch the rose with his hand. But how could the repeated inclinations have escaped our eyes, above all those very vigilant ones of Doctor Poso, who would have given anything to detect a *trick*?

The second episode, less sentimental but more comical, occurred with the tambourine. I mentioned that the tambourine appeared from behind the left curtain. Galeotti tried to grab it, but John (let's put it this way to make it short) snatched it from his hand and took it back behind the curtains. When it reappeared, Galeotti grabbed it again, but the other one would not let it go. There was an amusing struggle going on for several seconds during which one could distinctly observe the going back and forth of the sought-after tambourine, Galeotti holding it outside and John inside with a hand covered by the curtain. The struggle became so vigorous that a piece of wood was torn off from the tambourine. Finally the instrument ended up in Galeotti's hands and he got a bright idea. He stood up, lifted the tambourine with one hand against the curtain, and said: "John, play it!"

And the curtain grew restless, swelled out towards the tambourine as if pushed by a hand, and to our great surprise we all heard distinct rhythmic beats on the tambourine. It should be pointed out that Galeotti was standing up with his arm lifted, and Palladino was sitting. Supposing she had been able to liberate one hand (certainly not the one under my control, and Mrs. B. assured that neither the other one, but one never knows...), Eusapia could not have reached the tambourine from where she was sitting unless she had an enormously long arm, or unless her natural ones had been suddenly lengthened.

One of the times the tambourine was brought on stage, so to say, above Eusapia's head, I asked Poso to take it. He got up, approached it, and stretched out his arm. But the tambourine retreated a little at first, and then made a very fast movement as if to slap and reject the hand attempting to seize it. John seemed to be still in a bad mood.

Figure 21. Seventh session. Trace 1, signals obtained from the key placed in the mediumistic cabinet; trace 2, signals obtained from the key placed on the séance table; trace 3, signal connected with the key enclosed in the wire cage; trace 4, signals obtained from the Gaiffe magneto-electric machine; trace 5, time. Additional labeling: trace 1, Signal; trace 2, Signal; mid figure, Seventh session with E. Palladino Lab; trace 3, signal connected with the key enclosed in the wire mesh cage; trace 4, signal connected with the Gaiffe magneto-electric machine; trace 5, time; bottom, Seventh session with E. Palladino. Naples, May 13, 1907.

The two twin keys operated marvelously. By now Eusapia had learnt to make synchronous movements to perfection. As soon as the mediumistic hand started to make audible beats on the key inside, I placed the other key on the séance table and asked Eusapia to press both of them simultaneously. The result of this experiment is shown in the two following Figures (21 and 22). They present, in addition to traces to be

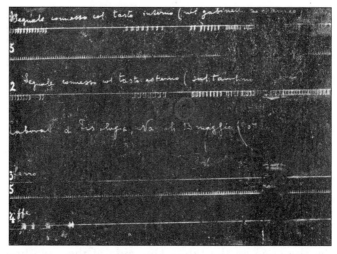

Figure 22. Seventh session. Continuation of traces 1 to 5 shown in Figure 21. Additional labeling: trace 1, Signal connected with the internal key (in the cabinet); trace 2, Signal connected with the external key (on the table); mid figure, Physiology lab, Naples, May 13, 1907.

described later, traces written by the pens of the two Desprez signals connected to the two spring keys (see the two upper lines separated by the time line). The traces show different groups of synchronous beats. The number of beats is not always the same in the two corresponding groups. In each group the beats started either on the key inside or on the key outside and then continued on the other key. However, the synchrony was always perfect. The beats showed a difference, one verifiable in the trace, the other by our ear. The first one (as also seen on the traces of the previous sessions) is that the mediumistic beats were faster and shorter, while those by Eusapia's visible hand were slower and thus longer. The second one reflected the force used for pressing, as judged from the intensity of the acoustic sensations felt by us. The external beats were very weak, hardly audible, while the interior ones were very loud, often violent enough to shake the table (the spring key got misplaced a bit). They sounded more like punches given to the key rather than mere beats.

All through the session we heard other loud beats on the tables inside and outside. They often sounded like punches given by a fist on the cage and at times by the cage on the table. One side of the cage had been fastened to the table by two robust wires in such a way that the other side could be raised and lowered. The telegraph key was fastened inside the cage, and the cover of the cage was not tightly fastened as in the previous session. If John had been clever enough, he could have simply uncovered the cage, put his hand inside, and pressed the key. We asked John several times to press that key but he failed. Apparently, the failure irritated him, since he then started to beat the cage against the table violently, and bang the cover so hard that it was bent a few centimeters. I said: "Uncover the cage and touch the key." "No," answered irritated Eusapia. She knew quite well that this meant a confession of her incapacity.

The trace of the signal connected to the key inside the cage showed no vertical sign.

Materializations were numerous and very important. Four times I clearly saw an enormous black fist coming out from behind the left curtain, which remained still, and advancing towards the head of Mrs. B. Immediately afterwards, the lady announced that she felt touched on her cheek, ear, and neck. The last time the fist remained outside so long that when I asked the sitters to turn their eyes in that direction, they clearly saw it. But what I am about to tell you now was probably the most striking event to me.

I felt an open hand tenderly seizing my neck from behind. Instinctively, I freed my left hand from Poso's right hand, placed it where I felt the distinct sensation of contact, and found the hand touching me. It was a large hand, neither cold nor warm, with bony, rough fingers, which vanished under my grip. It did not retreat, producing a rubbing sensation on my hand, but it vanished, 'dematerialized,' dissolved.

A bit later the same hand was placed on my head. I approached it with my hand, felt it, grabbed it, and again it dissolved, and vanished under my grip.

Still later, the same hand was placed on my right forearm without squeezing it. This time I put not only my left hand to the place I felt touched, but I also looked so that I could see and feel at the same time. I saw a human hand of natural color, and I felt with my hand the fingers and the back of a lukewarm, muscular, rough hand. *The hand vanished, and my eyes saw it retreat, describing an arc of a circle, as if entering back into Palladino's body.* I confess that I felt some doubt as to whether Eusapia's left hand had freed itself from my right hand to reach my forearm. Yet, at the same time I could verify that such suspicion was unfounded, since our two hands were in contact with each other in the usual manner. All the other phenomena I observed during these sessions may disappear from my memory, but this one will never vanish!

As it may be imagined, touches were numerous. It was enough to stretch a hand towards the curtain and ask it to be seized and the wish was immediately fulfilled. Only Doctor Poso was not pleased; he was only granted one short and light touch, just a push from inside the curtain.

The mysterious hand twice pinched my left knee with three fingers, and tapped twice on my shoulder with an open hand so hard that everybody heard the slaps. Lastly, I felt my head being hit by a hard object covered by the curtain. What was it? It was the vase where the roses had been. And after the hits, the water in the vase was poured out on the floor behind my shoulders while Eusapia said: "He meant to pour it over you, but then..." "Thank you," I answered, extending my hand to reach for the glass, but the glass had already vanished.

In the beginning of the session three rather big flames appeared, light blue and fading on the edges. Everybody saw them since they lasted several seconds. They looked like they were coming out from Palladino's head and rising in the air to the left with an undulating movement. They disappeared at a certain distance from her. Mr. B. himself confessed he had never seen them so clear and bright.

There were also two apparitions of human faces. They were not black but of natural color. They were fairly pale, almost diaphanous, and well lighted. Eusapia announced both apparitions. The first time a head appeared above her head but I did not see it, and I report what I was told by others. They asked, "Who is it?" And Eusapia answered in a thin voice: "It is Peppino!" The second time Eusapia leaned her forehead against mine and said: "Look!"

We looked and saw a very pale human head, clearly lit, sticking out behind the edge of the left curtain.

Not all of us agreed upon the interpretation of the vision. Mr. B. declared he had seen John King's head covered by a turban, as in previous sessions. Galeotti said that he had also seen something white wrapped around the head, which could have been the famous turban. I must confess that I only saw something pale and bright, perhaps due to my unfavorable position of having Palladino's head against mine. For me it corresponded to the upper third of a human face, a wide forehead. However, we all agreed upon the apparition itself, and on the place and time of its occurrence.

The most notable moving of objects during the session was that of the footstool with the dish of clay on top. After the dish was brought to the table, the footstool started to rap the floor so loudly that beats were heard at a considerable distance (the technician heard them while he was three or four rooms away). Eusapia stretched her left leg over my knees, and propped her foot against Poso's knee. This was an indication of some phenomenon needing much force. In fact, the footstool attempted to lift up, but fell back. I said to Eusapia: "Don't strain yourself. It is quite heavy. You cannot do it." "Yes, I can," she answered energetically.

And the footstool was up in the air, propping its corner on my right elbow. It remained in this awkward position for quite a while. Then, it succeeded to climb on the table with my help. But since it was too bulky, Mr. B. asked Eusapia to let him place it on the floor, and Eusapia consented.

Now I have to mention another very important phenomenon.

A small magneto-electric Gaiffe machine, modified to function as a rotator switch, had been placed on the table in the mediumistic cabinet. As can be seen in Figure 23, the two clamps of the box were holding two different wires instead of the usual excitatory wires. One of them was connected directly to the accumulator,

Figure 23. Seventh session. The Gaiffe magneto-electric machine.

while the other one reached the accumulator after going through a Desprez signal. Rotation of the handle produced several successive closings and openings of the electric circuit inside the box. As a result, the pen connected to the signal moved up and down, tracing white lines on the blackened paper of the cylinder (the pen connected to the recording Jacquet clock had been placed on the same cylinder). Clearly, to start the rotational movement of the instrument in the box and produce the sequential closing and opening of the electric circuit, it was necessary to turn the handle. But if you tried to turn it with a single hand without holding the box steady with the other hand, the box itself would be raised or displaced rather than producing the required movement, and the handle would at most turn only a few times. It is also clear that the number of closings and openings of the circuit per unit time varies, depending on the rate the handle is being turned, and so does the trace on the cylinder.

To our great surprise, after we gave Eusapia the necessary explanations and told her that the small box resembled the famous *carillon* musical box she had played many times during her sessions in Paris, the handle started to move and we all heard the characteristic noise made by the machine turning in the box.

Indeed, the trace provided uncommon evidence (see Figs. 21 and 22, lower lines). It showed that the handle was turned many times at variable intervals and with different speeds. The last time it was turned at a very high speed (see the lower trace of Fig. 22), and the cooperation of two mediumistic hands was indispensable. After the session, the box was found in the same position where it had been left.

The session ended with a short journey of the chair carrying the dish of mastic, that is with the same phenomenon it had started with. Under our eyes and in fairly bright light, the chair was dragged out of the cabinet with its three kilograms of mastic, and was pushed to our side of the curtain towards where Dr. Poso was sitting. No marks worth mentioning were found on the mastic, which was pressed only on one side where it showed minute marks of a fabric different from that of the curtain.

Palladino's urine was collected before and after the session.

A) Urine collected immediately before the session.

Quantity: cm^3 110.
Specific weight (+15°C): 1024.
Reaction: very acid.
Appearance: clear.
Abundant sediment found after leaving it
    about 20 hours in a glass.

Examination of the decanted urine;
Lowering of freezing point (Δ) = 1°.465.
Electric conductivity (K 37°C) = 271 × 10^{-4}
Albumin: 1.5 g per thousand.
Nitrogen total (from dealbumined urine):
    11.47 g per thousand.
Presence of glucose.
Excess of indican and alkaline and earthly
    phosphates.

Microscopic examination of the sediment:
Many mucus-pus particles
Many cells of the low genitor-urinary ducts
Initially, uric concretions, but after 20 hours
    several uric acid crystals are present in the
    sediment.

B) Urine collected immediately after the session.

Quantity: cm³ 90.

Specific weight (+15°C): 1024.

Reaction: very acid.

Appearance: clear.

Abundant sediment after 12 hours.

Examination of the decanted urine;

Lowering of freezing point (Δ) = 1°.480.

Electric conductivity (K 37°C) = 296 × 10⁻⁴

Albumin: 2 g per thousand.

Nitrogen total (from dealbumined urine):

12.15g per thousand.

Presence of glucose.

Excess of indican and alkaline and earthly

phosphates.

Microscopic examination of the sediment:

Same as for urine A.

Eusapia's pulse beats were taken several times before and after the session, but no notable differences were observed. She had from 80 to 90 beats per minute.

XII. Eighth Session (July 5, 1907).

Professors Bottazzi, Galeotti, and Scarpa were present in the usual room of the Physiology laboratory at 21:00. Also present were Mrs. Bottazzi; Dr. Gaetano Jappelli, professor in charge of physiological methods in this Royal University and assistant in the Institute of Physiology; and Dr. Gennaro d'Errico, assistant at the same Institute.

Figure 24. Eighth session. The mediumistic chain during a small levitation of the table. In the back, hands of Prof. Jappelli and Palladino touch each other, Palladino's wrist shows its fastening to the inextensible ribbon. Photo taken with a magnesium flash.

Figure 25. Eighth session. Another mediocre levitation of
the table photographed with a magnesium flash.

The mediumistic cabinet was the same as in the 7th
session. On the table there were, among other things,
a trumpet, a flower vase, an electric key, etc. A camera
was facing the séance table in the room, and a bag of
magnesium powder was placed in such a way that,
when an electric key was pressed at a given moment,
the platinum loop in the magnesium powder became
red-hot, yielding a flash of light.

We took photographs of two mediocre levitations of the table and of the sitters forming the chain (see Figs. 24 and 25).

Two iron rings were fastened to the floor near the two legs of the table on the *medium*'s side, and two strong ribbons bound to the rings were wrapped around Eusapia's wrists, each one with a double knot. Ribbons were sealed with lead under each knot the same way one seals railroad sacks or wagons. Sealing was done in presence of all of us. The seal carried the letters M.E. on one side and the word "Napoli" on the other (Fig. 26). Poor Eusapia! She submitted herself meekly to be tied up like a criminal, but not without protesting that she did it merely to play tribute to 'science,' while fully convinced of her honesty.

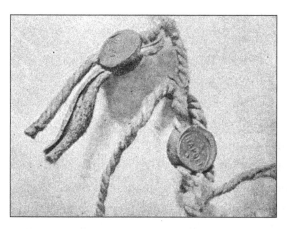

Figure 26. Eighth session. The seals on the ribbons' leads fastening Palladino's wrists.

We fixed the length of the ribbons in such way that her hands would never be able to reach any object in the cabinet, regardless of their position. Here were the distances measured before starting the session:

On Palladino's right side:

    distance from the right ring
    to Eusapia's wrist   1.07 m
    distance from the right ring
    to the flower vase   1.47 m
    distance from the right ring
    to the trumpet   1.50 m

On the left side:

    distance from the left ring
    to Eusapia's wrist   1.20 m
    distance from the left ring
    to the flower vase   1.89 m
    distance from the left ring
    to the trumpet   1.80 m

As it can be seen, the objects were at a distance of at least 40 centimeters on the right, and much farther from Eusapia's hands on the left.

At the maximal extension of ribbons and of Eusapia's fingers, and in their most favorable position, only the fingers of Eusapia's right hand could barely touch the edge of the table inside, which was fastened in the way described in the seventh session.

They remained at a distance of at least 12 centimeters from the flower vase and the trumpet.

Figure 27. Eighth session. The mediumistic cabinet and part of the séance room as they appeared at the end of the session. The ribbons tied to Eusapia's wrists are shown fastened to the floor by the sides of the séance table. Objects on the séance table were brought over from the table located in the mediumistic cabinet. The chair on the left was the chair where Eusapia was sitting.

The position of ribbons and rings with respect to the tables outside and inside is shown in Figure 27.

Ribbons were not extendable. For as much as we tried we could not stretch them.

At the end of the session, before cutting the loops around Eusapia's wrists, we all verified that the knots and the four seals were intact.

Jappelli made sure that the loops were tight around her wrists and her hands could not pass through them.

I'll tell in just a few words about the usual events which were reproduced with some modifications, and will describe in more detail three phenomena which were most relevant for us in the entire session.

A chair was brought twice onto the séance table, and a flask full of water also made the same aerial trip.

Two bells placed in the mediumistic cabinet were rung, thrown down, and rolled on the floor.

The heavy footstool often mentioned in this report was dragged for several centimeters from the corner where it was, and was raised and violently and rhythmically rapped against the floor. When I remember those very loud blows which thundered through the deserted rooms of the laboratory, and bear in mind that the *medium*'s wrists were tightly tied the way I have described, I cannot but smile at the unknown skeptical reader who shakes his incredulous head, and assumes that even this phenomenon was due to hallucination or cheating. It would be more appropriate for him to say that I was lying when writing these lines.

There were many touches on all of us, and many slaps by an open hand on Mrs. Bottazzi's back. Once I felt my left hand squeezed while I stretched it out for a little while on the back of Mrs. Bottazzi's chair. It was done by a warm hand about the size of Eusapia's hands. And Eusapia's hands were simultaneously in contact with her custodians' hands and were held by the bindings of her wrists.

Black hands appeared. At a certain moment Doctor d'Errico told me that a colossal forearm, black and somewhat diaphanous, was advancing on the séance table with a closed fist upwards.

I looked and saw it. The apparition lasted several seconds.

Finally I describe the three phenomena which I have hinted at.

The first event. Custodians of Eusapia's hands and feet were Prof. Jappelli on the left side and Mrs. Bottazzi on the right side (even if there was no need for it). They periodically informed us of the position and movements of the *medium*'s limbs. I was on the right side of my wife.

Eusapia told me: "Stretch your arm and put it on your wife's shoulders."

I obeyed and was soon given the trumpet from behind the curtain. I recognized it immediately by the touch, seized it, and placed it on the table.

The second event. Later on, without any warning we heard some kind of rubbing of the curtain on Eusapia's right side. The curtain was swelling a little, and from the same side out came the flower vase. Since the custodians (Mrs. Bottazzi and Doctor d'Errico) had orders not to interrupt the contact with Eusapia's hands for any reason, and I was the closest one on the chain, I extended my right hand, took the vase with the flowers and placed it on the table without spilling the water.

The trumpet and the flower vase were so far away that Eusapia's hands couldn't even touch them. Whether they were at a distance of ten, thirty, or fifty centimeters from the *medium*'s visible hands is not relevant. What is important is that it was absolutely impossible for her to reach them.

The third event. While Galeotti was the custodian of Eusapia's right hand, he clearly saw the *mediumistic doubling* of her upper left limb.

"Mind you," he said. "I see two identical left arms. One is on the table and is the one Mrs. Bottazzi is holding, the other seems to come out from Eusapia's shoulder, to approach Mrs. Bottazzi, touch her, and then return back and melt into Eusapia's body, vanishing. It is not a hallucination. I am awake and I am conscious of the two simultaneous visual sensations which I experience while Mrs. Bottazzi says she is being touched."

Some other objects, the electric key and the Marey kettledrum among them, were not touched, although we insisted. So we did not get their respective graphic traces. But this I need to explain a little more.

Eusapia said more than once that she was not able to touch them because they were too far, which was true. She was making confessions she had never made before, perhaps because of the intimate relation she had with all those present.

Referring to the extensions of arms she used for touching, moving, and transporting objects, she made us understand that these extensions vary in length during the sessions according to the greater or smaller 'fluid.' that is the mysterious 'mediumistic power' she feels within herself, and of which she is confusedly aware. These confessions could, however, be the result of our discussions where the mediumistic extensions were hinted at.

From the first session on, I had the intuition that the field of the *medium*'s actions has limits beyond which every motor phenomenon is impossible, and that these limits vary. Presently, the objects at the maximum distance of 20 or 30 centimeters or more from Eusapia's limbs cannot be touched or moved by her.

It seemed that her mediumistic power was at one time much stronger but, like I said, during these last years it weakened, and maybe it won't be long before she will lose it completely.

I know quite well that, irrespective of the measured distances, some meticulous person will say: "There you are again. Palladino only seized the objects closest to her. She never touched those farther away. Who knows, maybe she succeeded in seizing the closest ones despite her tied wrists!"

But how did she do it? The loop of the ribbon around her right wrist (the left one was not worth considering) was so tight that it did not allow any movement up or down, except a few centimeters at most. This was checked before and after the session. We put ourselves, one after the other, in Eusapia's place and became convinced that one does not reach farther than the edge of the table in the most favorable position of wrists and fingers, and under the maximal tension of the ribbon. Furthermore, it was not only a question of moving an object. To bring it over to us, one had to grab it. A large glass full of water cannot be moved with two fingertips without making water and flowers spill.

We confess that the results of this session had a favorable influence on our minds. They removed one of the many roots of doubt and uncertainty which torment the spirit of every calm and impartial observer of these unusual mediumistic phenomena.

XIII. General Considerations and Conclusions.

It is really unfortunate that in phenomena of this type the presentation of observed facts cannot be simple, plain, and objective, but must inevitably assume a polemic nature, and at times even personal aspects. The reason is to be found in the extraordinary nature of these phenomena, and in the fact that the human mind is more conservative than progressive. It follows that every new idea that differs too much from customary ideas is stirring and disturbing, and provokes a reaction which is stronger the more extraordinary the idea. The idea tries to pierce through and integrate, but it remains unrecognized, acknowledged neither as a sister nor as a daughter. To this reaction, certainly happening to everyone witnessing mediumistic[6] phenomena, are added the observer's extremely diverse ethical motives and different sentiments. They powerfully contribute to his shaping of opinion and judgment on the phenomena themselves, and moreover to his attitude towards the other observers. With regard to mediumistic events, the large majority of well-educated people consists of those who have never seen any. *Mediums* are much scarcer than jugglers or all kinds of magicians, and they do not work on stages. This is

---

[6] We need to keep this unfortunate word as we lack a better word which might replace it, and at the same time eliminate the primitive spiritualist meaning which originated from the role assigned to the *medium* in the production of mediumistic phenomena.

why only a few have been able to participate in mediumistic sessions. Naturally, this has a significant effect
on making these phenomena mysterious and putting
them in a bad light. This is not the fault of *mediums*. I
would rather say it might be better to blame the most
skillful magicians for not producing mediumistic-type
phenomena if what they do are only *tricks, vulgar
tricks,* as many believe. Is it possible that a magician
who is capable of stunning hundreds of people cannot
also make a table levitate or a chair move in such a
way as to make people believe that the table rises and
the chair moves by itself? The truth is that more than
one has tried, but was quickly caught as fraudulent.
Conversely, a well-known 'honest' magician who has
witnessed 'honest' mediumistic sessions confessed that
he could not have reproduced those phenomena. In
fact, mediumistic phenomena, or at least some of them,
belong to a different category from those produced by
jugglers to entertain the public. What people 'who
have not seen' mediumistic phenomena think of them
is really of no importance.

Those 'who have seen' can be divided into two
groups: one draws the conclusion that it is just a trick,
a vulgar trick (their favorite expression, stressing the
word 'vulgar'). They are the minority. The other group,
the majority, not having been able to detect any fraud
despite their rigorous surveillance, and knowing that
during the sessions they have experienced real (visible,

audible, and tactile) sensations, neither illusory nor hallucinatory, simply concludes that the so-called mediumistic phenomena are wonderful and not only deserve consideration, but also study.

It is worth inquiring why, out of two well-educated and worthy individuals attending the same or different mediumistic session, one is convinced in one way and the other in the opposite way.

If it is a question of different sessions, which is the most common case, the problem is simpler. Every biological phenomenon has a complex determinism, and its way of manifesting itself is not only influenced by external conditions, but also and prevalently by the inner conditions of a living organism. These conditions cannot be identical in every experiment, hence it is impossible to obtain identical results from experiments which are seemingly made under identical conditions. Let me give an example. You stimulate the vagus nerve with an electric current and observe the effect of the stimulation on the functioning heart, an organ whose operational regularity is comparable to that of a machine. The normal effect of such stimulation is the halt of cardiac movements. But every so often, one obtains the reduction in the frequency of beats or the decrease in the force of each beat, but the heart does not stop. Moreover, in some other cases, stimulation of the nerve makes a heart which was beating weakly or slowly or not at all, start to beat rhythmically for a short time. If somebody ignorant of physiology had seen such an experiment, and had later read in a treatise on this subject, under the chapter 'innervations of the heart,' that the stimulation of the vagus nerve stops the heart in diastole, what would he have said? "No, it is not true! The heart does not stop, on the contrary ..." But the physiologist, who has seen the heart stopping one hundred times and not stopping five times, may smile at such reaction. He knows that variable results may depend on the different conditions in which the heart and the nerve were found, on the intensity and frequency of stimulation, etc.

This also applies to the principal mediumistic phenomena, and in particular to those produced by Eusapia Palladino.

Poor Eusapia is not a machine, but a living organism. In hundreds of mediumistic sessions attended by trustworthy persons she has produced phenomena which leave no doubt with regard to their importance and reality, and to her honesty. On the other hand, in a few sessions phenomena have been scarce and weak, leaving the observers unsatisfied. And hence they were mistakenly led to believe that what was witnessed by others was of comparable intensity and nature, and greatly exaggerated by human credulity and simple-mindedness.

But this is a long way from declaring it was a fraud, and calling Palladino a cheat, a swindler. To state this, one needs to detect the fraud. Was Palladino ever caught cheating? It seems she was. Leaving aside unconscious *tricks* it seems that the only conscious, intentional *trick* Eusapia carelessly used more than once was to move an object in full light with the help of one of her hairs. If she were as smart as people say, she would not have done it. Because of that trick, she was reproached by Flammarion and others, but her intelligence is so low that she continues even now to amuse herself with the famous hair. She tries, so I believe, rather than to cheat, to make fun of somebody unsympathetic, hoping that the *trick* will pass as something real.

I also believe in another possibility. There are sessions or parts of session in which Eusapia is unable to produce any phenomena (for me this proves the reality of mediumistic phenomena when they do take place). These instances seem to occur more frequently now that she is getting older (she is already 53) and growing weaker, being ill more often than earlier, as shown by our urine analyses. Can any of us claim to be at any time equally ready or apt to work with the same energy and efficacy? But when she finds herself in such condition, it might be said that she should not attend a mediumistic session. This is true, but one needs to consider that she is often in other people's houses, where she has been invited to *work*. Quite often people coming from far away are there to see her. At times they are, let's say that too, inflexible like spectators at the theatre who, having paid for the ticket, expect to see and hear. If they leave unsatisfied, they grumble and throw insults like those I have hinted at above. Who could not admit that Palladino under such conditions, anxious to satisfy them to the utmost, sometimes yields to the temptation of fraud, producing with her natural hands and legs things that look like mediumistic phenomena? During our sessions, *we never discovered anything like it. Eusapia never used any kind of device to cheat. To the contrary, she never failed to alert us whenever she moved the table or the curtain with her visible hands.* But it cannot be absolutely excluded that under the conditions mentioned, she might have committed or is committing some minor fraud. In so doing, she appears to be unaware of the incalculable damage it would cause to her reputation and to the true mediumistic phenomena in the eyes of the vast majority of people. Unable to take part in such sessions, they need to trust the faithful reports made by those who were present to form whatever conviction.

To some extent this is also due to her limited intellectual development, and partly to her ignorance of the impression made on the public by the news regarding her frauds. In fact, she does not read newspapers, and does not like mediumistic phenomena to be discussed in her presence.

Be that as it may, it is highly unjust to deny the reality of mediumistic phenomena by just basing it on the few cases where Palladino's naïve and minor frauds were observed. We leave out the big frauds made by professional crooks who, once discovered in their wrong doings, have been compelled to stop. There are people who made poor observations only on few occasions and under unsuitable conditions. There are even worse people who started their observations under the prejudice of being confronted by fraudulent events. That is to say, they started out with a preset conviction or, still worse, with the arrogant intention of being right. Indeed, they have chosen to consider as idiots those who cannot believe in having been cheated, since this emphasizes their own superiority as observers and critics. All these people, and others who deny for even less noble reasons, will not have the power to diminish the value of the contrasting statements made by people holding such names as Crookes, Ramsay, Lodge, Lombroso, Richet, Flammarion, Luciani, or Morselli. These men are honest scientists whose fame cannot be shaken by the arrogance of a few for whom denying appears to be the sign of mental superiority.

To those who deny without having seen, and declare *a priori* the impossibility of the mediumistic phenomena, one has to reply: "First try to see, then we may argue."

Worthy of respect are those, and they are not a few, who refuse to see because they are afraid that what they observe might disturb their naturalistic convictions and their materialistic view of the world, a vision that they have reached through hard studies and long meditations. I do not share their fears, since what I have seen has not caused me any disturbance, nor shaken my naturalistic convictions. New knowledge has been superimposed on old knowledge, and although it has not been properly integrated with it, at least it has confirmed in my soul Leonardo's sentence: "Nature is full of infinite reasons that were never investigated!" After all, these gentlemen deserve as much respect as those believers who refuse even to learn the principles of natural sciences for fear of shaking or disturbing their religious faith.

I would be relentless with the small number of arrogant people who expect their few and poor observations to undo the vast number of observations made under different and often better conditions. The latter observations were made by people not inferior to them, but often superior in wit, experimental capacities, and sound character, proven by lifelong results. Arrogant people are readily surrounded by an ignorant and pretentious herd for the same reasons that a crowd is more likely to support the destroyer rather than the builder, the one who assembles obsolete reasons rather than the innovator. To all of them I would be relentless. But would it be worth it?

I am satisfied to tell them: "In what way are your senses superior to ours? What proof of your superior critical capacity have you shown? Where does your belief come from that only the few of you have seen clearly, and conversely that all of us have been seeing things, been cheated, never been able to detect the fraud? Is this only a mere conviction of yours? Then our conviction is at least as worthy as yours, with the difference to our advantage that our written reports demonstrate clearly that our observations were made at times under the best possible controls and furthermore we had a larger number of observations."

They keep repeating: "Everything is fraud, cheating." But when asked to explain how, and for what reasons they have come to this conclusion, to indicate by what means they have detected fraud, and how the *medium* cheats, they don't know what to say. We keep hearing the same nonsense again and again, that one has a clear intuition of fraud even if the means used by the *medium* to cheat cannot be pinpointed. It is like the unknown art of the magician, whose capacity nonetheless no one doubts. They keep repeating that the *medium* skillfully frees his hands from the custodian's and operates with an incredible skill and speed, as if custodians and other people present were lost in reverie to the point of not noticing anything. They add that the *medium* has got hidden mechanisms under his clothes, that he levitates the séance table by propping his foot under one leg of the table, and levering it by hands and arms, etc.

These are things that could have been mentioned thirty, twenty years ago, but not today when the observations of the mediumistic phenomena have considerably increased in number and become more refined.

And how to free the hands if they are uninterruptedly in contact with mine? By freeing the other hand, the one not in contact with me, of which I have no knowledge? But even admitting this, how could the *medium* handle objects close to me, for example the chair I am sitting on, definitely out of reach of the other hand? Furthermore, why should I be incapable of seeing the *medium*'s arm and hands doing these things, when I distinctly see the hands and arms of other participants, including those farther away? Eusapia's arms are not diaphanous. When they move, I see them and follow them with my eyes. I see her hands touching the curtain, her head on my head. Why should I not see them carrying a flask or a glass to the table, or creeping into the cabinet?

She is operating with her legs and feet! But when her legs are stretched over my knees, and her feet are propped against Jona's knees, or are held by Scarpa under the table, how could these feet drag out a table or a chair from the mediumistic cabinet?

How can Eusapia, poor little lady in poor health,

drag on the floor for thirty or forty centimeters my body, which weighs ninety kilograms, and the chair on which I was sitting, if she was using only one arm, the left arm (see the seventh session), since in no way could she have reached the back of my chair with her right hand?

Could she do it with very rapid movements that could not be noticed? But look! Some phenomena lasted entire minutes and our alert eyes were fixed on the moving object. How can one believe that nobody noticed Eusapia's moving arm going from it to the custodian's hand and vice versa?

People emphasize hidden mechanisms? But where were they, and of what nature? Scarpa and I have kept our right arms around Eusapia's back for a long time, while behind her back one or the other phenomena occurred in the mediumistic cabinet, and we have not seen or heard anything.

The pouring of liquid from the flask (sixth session) lasted many seconds in the mediumistic cabinet. We heard it. Eusapia's arms were in front of our eyes, immobile. Only her fingers were making lively movements felt by our hands.

We have seen the séance table levitate half a meter above the floor while we were around it, and nobody was touching it. Where were Palladino's props if she was standing like the rest of us with her hands in the chain? Were we blind?

Were we lost in dreams? Not at all! We were just chatting, even too much, and laughing and telling jokes to John King. I was quarreling with Galeotti, we were talking with Eusapia, we were getting up, sitting down, etc. Are these the conditions prompting illusion and hallucination? One is mistaken, having never participated in a 'spiritualistic' séance, if driven to believe that participants are immobile, quiet, and astonished 'like under the spell of a nightmare.' Galeotti said that 'spiritualistic' sessions are the most amusing occasions in the world. He has a point there, as one really sees extraordinary things, impossible to imagine, and useless to struggle to explain, since there is no way to do it.

After all, mediumistic phenomena are not just of one kind, they are not only kinetic phenomena. While it is permitted to suspect cheating in these cases, in other cases it is not. How would the *medium* produce those bright little flames which seem to light up over her head, and then go away slowly up in space, lasting long enough to be seen by everyone, no matter where he was? And what about apparitions of fists, colossal hands, and heads, so high up that not even the tallest of us could touch?

There is another phenomenon which absolutely excludes the possibility of fraud, even if it is a motor event. This is the occurrence of mediumistic events synchronous with movements of the *medium*'s visible limbs, as I have repeatedly insisted upon in this report. Mr. B. assured me that de Rochas had already described such synchrony in his book, before Barzini had mentioned it. We believe that we have produced indisputable graphic demonstration of this synchronism (see traces of the sixth and seventh sessions) with regard to the beats of two electric keys, but we have also established it in many other movements that could not be easily registered. When Scarpa held Palladino's feet in his hands, he always felt her legs moving in synchrony with ongoing displacements of the table or chair. As I mentioned, a kick to Jona's legs corresponded to the throw of the glass in the second session.

Very often Eusapia kept her hands, always in the chain with her two custodians, not on the séance table but on her thighs. Under these conditions, one felt her fingers to be continuously moving while inside the cabinet a key was beaten, liquid was poured from one flask to another, or some object was grabbed and brought outside. Now, as I simultaneously experience tactile sensations in my hand, and acoustic or visible sensations at a distance, how could I have any doubt crossing my mind about the distant phenomena not being operated by the same fingers I felt in mine? Not only fraud, but also illusion and hallucination from my part can be absolutely excluded.

Sometimes Eusapia felt like freeing one hand from mine, and I did not oppose it. She lifted it up and touched, for example, the curtain. I stared at it, never lost it from my sight, but never saw it entering the cabinet, or crossing the limit of the curtain. If at the same time a key was touched in the cabinet, or I felt a little touch on my chest or ankle, or a fist appeared far from me and Palladino, how could I have believed that the hand which I continuously saw was the same hand that was touching me, or beating the key, or appearing at a distance?

In conclusion, during our sessions neither fraud nor cheating ever occurred. I can affirm this with certainty, solemnly, also on behalf of all the other participants. Although we all differ with regard to studies, temperament (differences could not be greater than those among Lombardi, Scarpa, Jona, Galeotti, and mine), regions of birth (Veneto, Piemonte, Toscana, Umbria, Abruzzi, and Puglia, etc.), and age, nevertheless we all agreed and were convinced that the phenomena we had observed were never the product of fraud. They were true phenomena, however mysterious and elusive in their nature.

Attempts to give explanations have been many and futile. Having excluded fraudulent behavior, the genuine spiritualistic hypothesis does not seem to convince many people. According to this hypothesis, the spirit of a dead person invoked by the *medium* is present at mediumistic sessions, materializes, and generates phenomena observed by participants. To please Eusapia, we too pretended to believe in the intervention of her father John King, and we turned our questions and thanks to him. But as I have told you, this was done for the sole purpose of not contradicting her prejudices. All the more so because to behave in front of her like convinced spiritualists meant nothing to us.

For some observers the fundamental reason that excludes the genuine spiritualistic hypothesis is the indisputable fact that the mediumistic phenomena occur in strict dependence on the *medium*'s physiological and psychological organism. The psychic dependence is demonstrated by the fact that, although at times the phenomena are produced without the *medium* showing any apparent awareness, as when she is in trance, the *medium* often announces what she is producing, already has produced, or is going to produce. Don't we have to admit that taps on the electric key in the cabinet, occurring in synchrony with beats on the key outside and with movements of Eusapia's hand kept in mine, are closely dependent on her will while she, leaning over the table, is fully concentrated on this complicated and marvelous phenomenon?

For me, the physiological dependence is proven by the synchronism we recorded many times between the mediumistic motor phenomena and the movements in muscles of her arms, legs, shoulders, or neck, in brief of her entire person, which sometimes were barely perceptible.

Nevertheless, the spiritualistic hypothesis cannot be absolutely rejected and declared absurd, until it can be directly and definitely demonstrated that mediumistic phenomena are produced by a different, well-determined mechanism.

It is the marvelous fact of synchronism that has suggested to me the following representation of mediumistic phenomena.

Let us imagine that, in resemblance to the well-known phenomenon of split personality, the *medium* may experience, in addition to it, a splitting of his physiological personality which may be partial (of a single limb, etc.) or complete (apparition of entire persons).[7] Due to this, the *medium*'s organism would temporarily come into possession of, let's say, two left arms, two right arms, two heads, three or four legs, etc. These extra limbs seem to blossom out of the *medium*'s body (what Scarpa saw during the sixth session, and I more clearly saw during the seventh session would support my proposal), and remain 'materialized' for a shorter or longer time, either acting or not acting in such a state, and then vanish as if re-entering the same body they came out from. If one of these additional hands operates, it could do it only under the influence of volitional impulses coming from the *medium*'s psyche. These impulses, whether conscious

---

[7] I admit this not because of my personal knowledge, as we were never confronted by apparitions of entire persons during our sessions.

or unconscious, need be channeled through two kinds of conductors, one to the normal limb the other one to the additional, temporary limb. Possibly, volitional impulses are channeled in each type of limb in different proportions. It follows that synchronous movements may occur in the two kinds of limbs, and furthermore that the two movements may vary in force and velocity of execution. Their rhythm remains the same because the center of production is one, and one is the source of motor impulses.

I already mentioned that Eusapia's invisible limbs seem also to be endowed with sensitivity. This cannot be surprising if it is assumed that they differ from the so-called natural limbs only with regard to the period of existence. The phenomenon of peripheral projection of sensations suggests that those felt by the additional limbs might also, simultaneously, be localized in the *medium*'s homologous limbs.

The representation (take note that I do not speak of *explanation*) may seem daring, but certainly agrees with the mediumistic phenomena we observed. It is a radical concept, but not illogical in any way. While this is just a representation, the so-called spiritualistic hypothesis is rather a true explanation which, perhaps for this reason, is satisfying to the majority of observers and acceptable to most people.

The splitting of physiological personality corresponds to the splitting of psychic personality, which is one of the most accepted facts in the science of human psyche.

With regard to the proposed physiological splitting, perhaps one could find somebody ready to admit that such a concept is not completely out of line from what we know. Someone might even dare to add that such event is continuously occurring in nature under various forms. The difference is that natural forms are in the domain of our research methods, and thus are considered well known despite our ignorance of their profound determinism. Conversely, this particular type of splitting, I would call it mediumistic, has so far evaded our investigation so that it seems even more mysterious. From a certain point of view, aren't there different forms of physiological splitting, for example the generation of new living beings from their parents, the multiplication of unicellular organisms, or the regeneration of amputated limbs in inferior organisms?

The time required for splitting varies, and so does the time required by organisms and regenerated organs to exist. But huge differences are already present between the time needed by dividing bacteria and the time necessary to regenerate an organ. The lifetime of *Ephemera* is much shorter than that of a century-old oak tree.

Organisms and living organs are steady-state energetic systems of extremely varied duration. While they last, they are revealed to our senses by certain characteristics that we attribute to matter. As a result, we say that they are made of matter and of the energy which any system contains. In this regard, mediumistic limbs in no way differ from those we are used to calling natural limbs; in fact, they appear to us, as natural limbs do, for their visual, tactile, and thermal sensations, and for the resistance they elicit in us, for the movements they make, for the sounds they generate, etc.

For these reasons, let me repeat, a possible representation of mediumistic phenomena appears to me as the one I have just presented, which can be summarized in the following words:

Mediumistic phenomena are not mere hallucinations of those attending sessions known as spiritualistic sittings. They are biological phenomena depending on the MEDIUM's organism. If they are such, they occur AS IF they are operated by the extensions of natural limbs or by additional limbs stemming out of the MEDIUM's body, and returning and dissolving into it after variable times. During those periods they reveal themselves by the sensations they elicit in us as limbs in no essential way different from natural limbs.